Tarot Games

Tarot Games

45 Playful Ways to Explore Tarot Cards Together

A New Vision for the Circle of Community

Cait Johnson and Maura D. Shaw

Illustrated by Durga T. Bernhard

HarperSanFrancisco
A Division of HarperCollinsPublishers

TAROT GAMES: *45 Playful Ways to Explore Tarot Cards Together.* Copyright © 1994 by Cait Johnson and Maura D. Shaw. All rights reserved. Printed in the United States of America. No part of this book may be used or reproduced in any manner whatsoever without written permission except in the case of brief quotations embodied in critical articles and reviews. For information address HarperCollins Publishers, 10 East 53rd Street, New York, NY 10022.

Preface © 1994 Vicki Noble
Illustrations © Durga T. Bernhard

FIRST EDITION

Johnson, Cait.
   Tarot games: 45 playful ways to explore Tarot cards together / Cait Johnson and Maura D. Shaw ; illustrated by Durga T. Bernhard. — 1st ed.
   p. cm.
   Includes bibliographical references.
   ISBN 0-06-250964-0 (pbk. : alk. paper)
   1. Tarot. 2. Interpersonal communication—Miscellanea. 3. Interpersonal relations—Miscellanea. 4. Mental healing. I. Shaw, Maura D. II. Bernhard, Durga T. III. Title.
BF1879.T2J65 1994
133.3'3424—dc20   93-48283
                                                     CIP

94 95 96 97 98 ❖ RRD(H) 10 9 8 7 6 5 4 3 2 1

This edition is printed on acid-free paper that meets the American National Standards Institute Z39.48 Standard.

We dedicate this work to the Goddess,
who clearly supported this project in so many
synchronous and magickal ways.
May feminine value continue to rise and heal this planet.

Contents

Preface: *Mending the Circle* by Vicki Noble ix

Introduction: A New Vision for the Tarot 1

Chapter 1: Beginning Circle Games 7

Listening to the Wisdom Within 7
Sacred Play 8
Some Cautionary Advice 9
Preparation of the Inner Self: Some Helpful Tools 10
The Right Deck 13
About Shuffling 14
A Final Helpful Hint 15

Chapter 2: Games for a Small Circle (Traditional-type Spreads for
One, Couples Games, and Games for Two or Three Players) 17

Magic Wand 19
The Snake 21
Cosmic Match 23
Sacred Cave 25
Five Seasons 28
Iris 30
Deep Water 32
The Lovers' Game 34
Completion 37
Feelings and Needs 38
Balance 40
Family Portrait 42
Fish 44
Wheel of Life 45
Birthday Game 48
Tea Party 49
Prosperity 50

Chapter 3: Games for a Larger Circle (Three or More Players)   53

    Empress   55

    Seed Sowing   56

    Gifts and Secrets   59

    Magic Carpet   60

    Blind Faith   61

    Symbol Seeker—A Magickal Treasure Hunt   62

    Maiden, Mother, Crone   64

    Acting It Out   65

    Sword Warrior   66

    Body of the Goddess   69

    Earth, Water, Fire, and Air   70

    Mask   72

    Comforter   74

    Sun, Moon, Star   75

    Dreaming the Dark: In Honor of Starhawk   76

Chapter 4: Games Especially (But Not Only) for Children   79

    Build a House   81

    Animal Friends   82

    Autumn Leaves   84

    Plant the Seed   85

    Through the Door   86

    Wishing Well   88

    Guardian Angel   89

    Circle of Protection   90

    Quest   91

    Who Are You?   92

    Helping Hand   93

    Pathway   94

    Completing the Circle   96

Tarot Resources   99

Further Reading   103

Acknowledgments   109

About the Authors   112

Mending the Circle

Tribal cultures around the world have woven into their social fabrics the necessary resources that people need to communicate interpersonally, to share traditional stories and beliefs, to resolve personal, family, or community conflicts, and to simply while away the dark hours during the winter. Western culture on the other hand, and American culture in particular, has developed a much more linear and work-oriented society that allows us very few channels to simply reflect on ourselves and one another. When we do, we tend to think and worry over our problems without having any effective personal tools for resolving those problems. And our increasing isolation from others, due to our extreme mobility and the isolation of individual nuclear families, leads to further anxiety. Many of us live without the relief and help of an extended family or familiar community.

Tarot is one method for reclaiming some sense of the sacred community we have lost, and it is appropriate for us to use, since our North American roots go back to medieval Europe, where the Tarot was "invented" and popularized. Actually, the game of Tarot was probably carried into Europe by the migrating Dravidian peoples of India, after they were disrupted by the Indo-Aryan invasions so many millennia ago. You can imagine then that some remnant of the ancient Indus Valley Goddess-worshiping culture is present symbolically in the Western Tarot tradition. That was certainly my impression when I first laid eyes on a Waite deck!

The bright images contained in many Tarot decks—pictures that heal and guide, awakening the intuition and opening the ability to channel for one-self and others—form a picture language that is universally available. Tarot is appreciated as a medium of communication that can tell us much about life on this planet. Of course, the images of the earlier tradition were rigidly bound by a single culture. In the Motherpeace deck Karen Vogel and I created, we broke free from this by making the deck round, instead of rectangular, and including images of the Black, Brown, and Red people of this earth along with the White. I remember taking the Motherpeace deck to Mexico in 1983, shortly after its publication, and showing it to Indian children we met on the streets. They loved the images! No need for texts explaining the meanings or how to use them—these kids understood them perfectly, just as children in the United States do.

I have always advised my students that, for the best or most natural read-ings of the cards, they need to find the child inside and read as if they were eight years old. "Sacred play" I called it in the *Motherpeace Tarot Playbook,* taking my cues from the kids who saw the cards in the early days after publi-cation. Yes, oracles and prophesy are serious, of course; but on the other hand, playing with the cards is fun and relaxing, an easy way to contact the inner Self. Anybody who has visited a Native American community on the day of a sacred dance or ceremony has experienced this same easygoing and playful approach to something that is taken very seriously by everyone.

Children today are watching more television than any of us would have ever imagined. A disproportionately large number of the images they see are violent and pornographic to some extent, teaching them negative values that most parents would not approve of. Advertising is bad, but cartoons are the worst offenders, showing more acts of violence than even prime-time evening shows. Not only are many of the images themselves negative and harmful, but the process of television viewing in itself is not neutral. The rays that the television sends out hypnotize the viewer, opening the unconscious mind and making it all the more susceptible to the incoming pictures and ideas. Television is by far the most powerful medium for hammering home the messages of these programs and commercials.

When I first began to open psychically in the late seventies, I experienced an organic cleansing process that seemed to be related to the unhealthy images I had "ingested" from the culture. These old, obsolete images were sexist, racist, consumer-oriented, and mechanistic. In my meditations and trace journeys, these images were released, and I was able to let go of them, understanding that they didn't really have much to do with me as a person in my own right. During this time I began to draw my own pictures of the way I imagined ancient cultures to be, and especially of how women and children might have lived in those earlier times when we had peace all over this planet. I guess you could say these were "visionary" pictures, since I was imagining something from the past that would help me to live better in the future.

From these first drawings of mine, Karen Vogel and I fashioned the Motherpeace Tarot deck. Our intention was to create positive, healthy, healing images of people living everyday life in ways that are not violent and do not harm the soul. We intended these life-affirming images to help people as they cleansed their psyches of negative, hurtful images by replacing those images with powerful, positive ones. Our many years of scholarly research went directly into these playful, folksy pictures, which any child can read and understand clearly. And truly, when children "read" the cards, they do so with insight and phrasing that duplicates almost verbatim what I wrote in the Motherpeace book! Behind and under all the symbols and pictures in the cards are sacred teachings, including shamanism, Buddhist concepts, and Native American ways of life.

Psychic teachers say that when we release old "stuff" from the psyche, a vacuum is created that must be filled with something or else the old image will return and lodge in its familiar place in the unconscious. So, for instance, when cleaning out old images or beliefs, you could "put a rose" in the empty place, in order to keep it clear. The Motherpeace cards, as well as other spiritually based decks, offer new, positive images that help to replace the old, ugly ones we have taken into ourselves through advertising and other forms of cultural propaganda. Simply using a Tarot deck in this way constitutes "psychic healing."

Tarot is a powerful medium of communication, just as television is. A Tarot deck doesn't send rays into the viewer, but it is alive with magic, and I'm sure it emits a vibration that can be transmitted and felt. If a person opens himself or herself to the Tarot images, the pictures enter the unconscious and do their work. In working with the cards, it is not necessary to understand the intellectual underpinnings of the tradition of Tarot, or of any of the teachings of the Western magical tradition that includes Tarot. Rather, a person can simply "read" what she or he sees or feels from the images themselves, just as the authors of this book suggest. As long as a person uses a Tarot pack with full pictures, the pictures tell the whole story and provide all the necessary information.

You needn't use the Tarot in a traditional way, as the authors of *Tarot Games* have shown, but you can play and experiment with many different and varied forms of "readings" and "games." I often teach my students to simply tell the story from the picture, the way they would read a dream image or a poem. Then they apply the information to their real-life situation, and the reading is done. All of these Circle Games are ways of using the cards to communicate and to break down the socially induced barriers that have developed between and among people. Surely none of us wants to be as isolated as we have become in Western culture, thinking our solitary thoughts and getting our stimulation from the television set.

The wonderful thing about using these simple games and "reading layouts" is that they catalyze the deeper processes taking place between people. This in itself is healing. In many situations, just the opportunity to express our feelings and share our ambiguities with others is enough to make us well. I remember when my teenage daughters were growing up (during the time I was creating the Motherpeace images); they were quite uninterested in anything "uncool" like discussing deep feelings or values with adults. Yet they and their friends very much enjoyed playing with the cards, which always led organically to these deeper expressions of value and sharing. I even took the cards into their junior high school and taught an extracurricular class for a while.

Tarot cards are so truthful and direct, it can be embarrassing to use them in contexts where people's feelings are normally kept under wraps. Yet they break the ice so gently and with so little fanfare that most people open to their messages and are able to "hear" things they would not normally tolerate. These Circle Games are aimed at friends, couples, and groups of people who trust and care about one another. They are intended to facilitate conversations that would be difficult if done directly and without a mediation tool. The games themselves are deceptively simple, which allows the players to be creative and experimental, evolving and personalizing the games and readings even further.

I know that in my life, using the cards when there is conflict in relationships has been enormously helpful. Just think about it for a moment. You and your partner are angry with each other and in disagreement over some trivial (or even serious) incident. The more you discuss the issue, the madder you get, and still there is no apparent way to come to an agreement. You can't go on without resolving the problem, but you can't seem to figure out how to resolve it without some outside intervention. Therapy isn't always available, and besides, it costs a lot. Your Tarot cards are right there, and they are the perfect helper—inexpensive and nonjudgmental!

Magically, the cards tend to reveal the shadows and weaknesses of both you and your partner or friend. They don't take sides. They show strengths as well as failures, and they point to ways of helping yourself, each other, and the situation. They are tricky and witty, finding clever ways of getting around whatever attachment you have to your own perception of reality. Because the cards love you both, you are encouraged to open to "the other." Somehow, neither of you turns out to be right! If you support your Tarot work with incense, ritual, and prayer, then the intervention is even stronger. Using *Tarot Games* in this way can be like coming to an ancient temple together and asking the Goddess for help or healing.

I almost always use the Motherpeace cards to open my workshops on healing. The women who come to the circle are usually strangers, and we need a way of building trust and opening the door for the deep work we will be doing together, usually only for a short time, two or three days. When the women in the circle choose a Motherpeace image and read it with a partner, they experience immediately the magic of the invisible forces of healing. (This would be true with other decks as well.) It is truly amazing when a perfect stranger, in love and trust, is able to look at a picture on a Tarot card and tell you some truth about yourself and your current situation. It is a bonding activity in the most sacred and yet simple way. Laughing and crying together, people realize they are not alone.

Sometimes I teach methods of reading the Tarot, using the rules of the tradition and certain "spreads," or reading layouts. But more frequently, I ask that my students learn to pull cards from the deck at random, in response to a question or issue they have on their minds. The more you study and learn the tradition of Tarot, of course, the more you can ostensibly bring to your work as a counselor or helper, if that is your calling. But sometimes I see people getting overly serious (or even pious) in relation to the rules of the game, a rigidity that gets in the way of actually using one's intuition. These Circle Games are fun and easy and are not to be taken too seriously, and as such, they will allow the intuition to play freely among friends and acquaintances.

I'm afraid I often break one of the cardinal rules of the Western magical tradition by bringing my cards out for fun at parties or other "nonserious" gatherings. They are so much fun! People always gather around out of curiosity and interest, and then they find themselves opening their hearts and minds to the magic inherent in the deck. This kind of activity pulls people together, rather than pushing them apart, and it links people horizontally rather than pitting them against one another in competitive ways, as so many party games tend to do. For those of us who remember our parents playing tense games of poker and bridge around the table, these Circle Games can restore a sense of familial closeness that is otherwise lost to us in the modern age.

I like the variety of readings available in *Tarot Games* and the different ways they focus on a question or situation. I use my own cards almost every day to ask questions, to solve problems, to get guidance, and just generally to relax and ground myself. But I hardly ever use a full, formal reading layout. It's too much trouble, and it's not usually necessary. I like to shuffle the cards, feel them in my hands, and play with them by myself and with other people. I like to use the cards to make people comfortable and open things up. I consider them a tool for socializing and making peace in our world. I believe we need sacred tools that will mend the broken circle of humanity before it's too late for us and other living things.

When my daughter Brooke was fourteen, a friend of ours invited her to attend a conference in Las Vegas on ways to bring an end to the underground nuclear testing that goes on there and in other places in the world. Brooke was very interested in the subject, inspired and passionate as only a youngster can be, and she wanted something to come of the conference. At the last plenary session on Sunday afternoon, the participants were trying to summarize what had gone on and what conclusions they could arrive at together. Our friend tells the story of how Brooke watched the adults bumbling about, attempting to come to some sort of effective agreement but instead arguing about methods and approaches, unable to find the desired unity.

Finally, Brooke pulled out her Motherpeace deck and offered to use it to help the group come to a peaceful conclusion. Using her own simple intuition, she was able to bring a kind of healing to the larger group process through the message given by the cards. My friend was very impressed, and Brooke was pleased with her own unexpected authority in the situation. Physical anthropology has observed that evolutionary innovations among animals often come through the impulses of adolescent members of the group, so it is not really surprising that a teenager could cut through what the adults in a human group were unable to see.

Maybe *Tarot Games*, which guides people of all ages on how to use the Tarot but has a whole section focused on games for children, will be a vehicle for the evolutionary growth we so desperately need. In any event, it should provide hours of fun and sharing for adults and children alike. Get a friend, your favorite Tarot cards, and as the authors suggest, pour yourself a cup of mugwort tea, light a beeswax candle, and start asking your questions. Good luck, and have fun!

Vicki Noble,
author of *Motherpeace: A Way to the Goddess Through Myth, Art, and Tarot*

A New Vision for the Tarot

Tarot is reaching mainstream acceptance as a powerful tool for life change and personal healing. The substance of this book is a direct outgrowth of the pioneering work on Tarot by such authors and teachers as Vicki Noble, Rachel Pollack, and Mary Greer, and we want to say at the outset that we owe them, and many others, a great debt of gratitude. But what we envision here is a very new and different approach to the Tarot, maybe even a revolutionary one.

Traditionally, the Tarot is a fairly solitary pursuit. Either you seek out a Tarot counselor who "does" the cards with you, or you sit face to face with the cards, alone. What we offer here is a way to use the Tarot with others in an interactive way that will benefit everyone, give valuable information about each player's life and self, and weave webs of connectedness that strengthen and nourish all the participants.

Next to dialoguing with dreams, Tarot has always been the best tool we have for connecting with inner wisdom and a sense of higher power and purpose. Now we offer an expanded way to use the cards, embracing Tarot as a gentle approach to group therapy, as a couples counseling tool, and as a healing ally that encourages transformation and change, not only for individuals but for groups as well.

All of this sounds very serious—and it is—but the form that we were inspired to choose is that of games, connecting us with our own sense of sacred play. The forty-five games in this book, which we call Circle Games, are intended to be played—they're fun—but they offer play with a purpose, in contrast to the meaningless and superficial stuff that usually passes for fun in our society. Remember party games? Card games? Many of us grew up watching our parents play bridge or poker, and although the games were supposed to be "fun," after a few hours of play the air was often filled with tension and competitiveness. Now we embrace a happier vision: of our children watching us playing these Circle Games with our friends and seeing us gently move into self-awareness and loving closeness; of our children playing these games with us and finding serenity and self-empowerment; and of all of us having a wonderful time.

Circle Games offer a way for those new to the Tarot to begin exploring and playing with the cards. As we have worked with the games, teaching and facilitating their play at workshops and gatherings, we have seen how beginners, initially tense and unsure about their abilities, have blossomed into greater self-confidence after playing. The games give them a nonthreatening way to bring Tarot into their lives.

If you feel a little daunted by the Tarot, you are not alone. Seventy-eight cards are a lot to tackle, and many beginners have an underlying belief that there is a "right" way to do things, known only to the experts. This can cause a lot of anxiety. But when you play Circle Games, you learn, painlessly, by doing. The process is a lot of fun—and the end result is greater understanding, not only of your life and of your inner self but of the cards as well.

For those of us who have been working and playing with the cards for years, Circle Games offer a whole new dimension. We have had seasoned Tarot users come up to us after a workshop and say, "This is great! I'm going to use some of these games with my Women's Spirituality group" (or my Full Moon circle, or whatever). They are a way for us to dialogue, share, get closer, and deepen together.

It is no secret that, unless we learn to work together cooperatively, the bugs will inherit the earth. This book, in its own way, provides tools to begin the process of trust-building, of group bonding, and, most important, of accessing real self-knowledge. A true understanding of our inner selves is the first step in feeling our essential kinship with one another on this infinitely dear and threatened planet. So it is in this spirit, which we call Goddess consciousness, that we offer this book.

The Goddess, as many of us are fond of pointing out, is rising. Her way of relating and being in the world is beginning to grow, pervading our diseased society, becoming accepted and even longed for. As Starhawk says in *The Spiral Dance:* "Mother Goddess is reawakening, and we can begin to recover our primal birthright, the sheer, intoxicating joy of being alive. We can open new eyes and see that there is nothing to be saved *from*, no struggle of life *against* the universe, no God outside the world to be feared and obeyed; only the Goddess, the Mother . . . whose winking eye is the pulse of being—birth, death, rebirth—whose laughter bubbles and courses through all things and who is found only through love."

The way of the Goddess gives us hope for our troubled species and for our mother, Earth. Goddess consciousness affirms the sacredness of Earth and of our bodies, connects us firmly and joyously to the cyclical dance of the seasons, and urges us to live in harmony with one another and with all creatures. The Goddess teaches us that all things are filled with spirit, reanimating our world. She shows us the nature of magick and urges us to create and respond with our whole selves to the magick of nature. And she reminds us that women, as creators, connectors, and the bearers of life, are holy.

After centuries of patriarchal oppression, so damaging to the true nature of men as well as to women, the Goddess offers us a way to heal and find wholeness together.

We have taken the Goddess's primary symbol, the circle, for the theme of this book. Circles recall the shape of the moon, the Earth, a baby's head crowning at birth. Circles have no hierarchy: When a group sits in a circle, all members are equal. In many magickal systems, a circle is cast to protect all those within its boundaries—and to contain the power raised inside. Circles are symbols of wholeness and possibility.

Whatever the size of your circle, Circle Games offer a key to the Tarot that can unlock wondrous possibilities for you.

Whether you are just starting out on the path of earth-connectedness or have been traveling it for a while, we hope that there will be something here that speaks to you and inspires you to explore and play. We hope that you will be empowered to share what you find here with others, and that this ripple in the stream will form ever-widening circles, for the good of all.

Blessed be.

Chapter 1

Beginning Circle Games

*t*his chapter introduces you to the magickal world of Tarot and will help you enter into the playful spirit of Circle Games. It includes some important advice about playing with others and offers some helpful ideas for preparing your inner self. We recommend that you take a few minutes to read it through before beginning to play.

If you are entirely new to the Tarot and feel that you need more substantial guidance, the Further Reading section at the end of this book will give you a solid grounding. Although this book is not a basic manual of Tarot, the games themselves are a gentle way to begin your exploration of the cards. Trust your ability to see what you need to see in each image shown on the cards. While it is true that you can spend a lifetime studying the traditional meaning and esoteric significance of the cards, your unique vision is what is most important for you.

Listening to the Wisdom Within

Much of what is wrong with our world today stems from a terrible alienation from, and loss of, the inner self. Life is our greatest gift, but when it is lived apart from the deep self, it can become a burden. Rather than being encouraged to communicate with and understand our inner selves, we are trained from birth to look outside ourselves for answers: We continually give our power over to others—the boss, the minister, the psychic, who tells us what will be. Circle Games are a very conscious part of the movement toward the inner self, where true wisdom lies. We see this active reclamation of our inner power as a healing tool for the self and for the planet. By embracing the part of the self that is connected to whatever we conceive the Higher Power to be, we embrace our ability to heal and empower ourselves, one another, and our world.

Most of us have spent years ignoring or suppressing our inner voices. When we finally tell our inner selves that we are ready to listen, the messages just come pouring through! It is as simple as relaxing, stilling the superficial voices that natter on in our minds, and opening to the experience. We have included some exercises and other ideas in the "Preparation of the Inner Self" section below to help you do this.

Sacred Play

Far from trivializing the magick of the cards, Circle Games are based on the idea that play can be sacred and meaningful, that the deepest wisdom can be discovered through laughter and shared enjoyment. One of the most important things we have found in teaching and playing these games is that deep seriousness and an impish sense of fun can coexist beautifully. As Vicki Noble points out in *Motherpeace:* "When you 'play' with Tarot cards, something broader opens out—consciousness expands into a realm rarely travelled by most of us. It happens, not when you are willing something to happen, but at that moment when you forget yourself and discover something larger than ego and daily reality. This 'space' has been called 'magic' and 'sacred.' . . . All forms of sacred play are direct routes to the Goddess and the pure wisdom of the lotus blossom."

Some Cautionary Advice

While there are no strict rules to follow when playing Circle Games, there is a code of ethics, as there must be with any pursuit that involves other people and the deeper reality that exists beneath the surface of all life. It is vital to keep this code in mind. First of all, the future is never graven in stone. While the cards will tell what is brewing for us, the whole point of doing a reading or playing a game is to give us the information we need to make choices that will shape a bright and joyful future. Distrust people who look at the cards and tell you, "Here's what will happen. There's nothing you can do." The cards are *all* about what you can do to change things if you don't like the way they are stacking up.

Sometimes a card will appear upside down in the game: These reversed cards appear for a reason and need to be interpreted in their reversed position. When a reversed card comes up, first look at it upright and then try to imagine how that meaning might be opposed or softened. Another possible way to interpret a reversed card is that the meaning is hidden from you at this time. Often, cards that were reversed in an earlier game will begin to appear upright as you work through the issue they represent in your life.

Then there are the scary cards: Most decks have a few, and their appearance in a game can cause some tension. We have found that approaching these cards as valuable teachers, rather than as portents of doom, is healing and helpful. If you heed the warning in the cards, chances are that you can avoid the pitfalls. But if you can't, remember that life is full of events that seem disastrous or negative at the time; growing into graceful alignment with your self means trying to see the ally hidden in the pain. Don't lose heart—look for guidance and for the lessons you are meant to learn in each experience.

A note on the Death card: This is *rarely* a warning of an actual, physical death. We like to think of the image in the Motherpeace deck—this Death card shows a snake shedding its skin. We must shed old, outgrown ways of being in order to become our best possible selves. We must ask, In what ways do we fear letting go? To be reborn, old constrictions must die. Celebrate the transition!

Most important, since these games are meant to be played with others, it is vital to maintain a sense of personal integrity and responsibility. If you harbor a grudge, or if you feel unable to approach the cards in a healing and positive way, we strongly advise a period of solitary play.

Preparation of the Inner Self: Some Helpful Tools

Simply focusing on the cards will help to relax, ground, and center the self. But we have found that a short ritual, a guided meditation, or a moment of focused stillness is a helpful ally before beginning any play with the Tarot.

Ritual is any series of repeated actions performed with intention. A short ritual, done every time you begin a game, is the most direct way to tell your inner self that you are ready to listen. Most of us use ritual in our daily lives without being aware of it. For instance, choosing the same favorite mug each day for your tea or coffee break is a kind of unconscious ritual that helps to set aside that time to relax and nurture the self. When created consciously, ritual becomes a powerful way to connect with the higher powers and our own higher/deeper self. Opening the door of magickal consciousness is something ritual has been known to do for centuries: It speaks a language that our mysterious selves understand immediately.

Here is our favorite short, simple, but effective ritual, which we use before every game.

> After mixing the cards, rub your hands briskly together, then hold them a few inches above the cards. Take a moment to feel the energy tingling in your hands. Then picture the energy flowing into the cards. Take a deep breath, let it go, and then ground the energy by placing your hands palms down on the floor or the table.

You can invent more elaborate rituals, involving props if you like. We sometimes enjoy setting the scene for Circle Games with beeswax candles, special incense, and a silk cloth on the floor to receive the cards. You can cast a circle using salt and water or by walking around the playing space with a smudge stick: The scent of burning sage and cedar purifies the air—and smells wonderful. You can invoke the elements, or the Goddess, or the spirit of the Tarot, with whatever words feel powerful to you. The Further Reading section includes several books filled with fine information on creating ritual, but your imagination and your need are your best guides.

Another way to bring yourself into magickal time is with a guided meditation, which works to make the self feel safe, focused, and relaxed. If you want to learn more about guided meditation, read Shakti Gawain's book *Creative Visualization*. And there is a wealth of wonderful material in Diane Mariechild's *Mother Wit* and in Starhawk's *The Spiral Dance*.

We have included two meditations here. The first focuses on the need for protection and involves the players in the elemental energies contained in the Tarot suit cards. The second is sometimes considered the Grandmama of all guided meditations. Transformative on many levels, Tree of Life heals and energizes the self. Both meditations may be done silently, or one member of the group can slowly read them aloud, leaving pauses between the sentences for images to take shape.

Elemental Protection

Sit comfortably, eyes closed. Take a few deep, cleansing breaths. Be aware of your breath and the intake of life and energy, the exhalation of tension and negativity. As you continue to breathe slowly and fully, begin to imagine that you are seated on a large, flat rock, smooth and warmed by the sun. Feel the peaceful presence of the rock, its firmness, its safe foundation for your sitting. Know that its spirit, dancing an earth-dance, protects you and keeps you safe.

Now imagine that you can hear the sound of a stream, splashing and murmuring in its channel near you. The stream sparkles in the sun. The sound of its song washes away any troubles or anxieties and leaves you feeling clean and peaceful. Know that the spirit of the stream, dancing a water-dance, protects you and keeps you safe.

Now imagine that a small, round campfire burns quietly near you, warming you, the sweet smell of its woodsmoke invigorating and cheering you. Know that the spirit of the fire, dancing a fire-dance, protects you and keeps you safe.

And now imagine that a warm, scented breeze stirs your hair, gently blowing away your fears, gently inspiring and refreshing your mind. Know that the spirit of the wind, dancing an air-dance, protects you and keeps you safe.

Feel yourself surrounded, protected, and embraced by earth, and water, and fire, and air. Take a deep breath and open your eyes.

Tree of Life

Sit comfortably with your spine straight. Close your eyes and breathe deeply, becoming aware of your breath. As you breathe in, feel yourself drawing in clear light and energy, pure energy. See each out-breath as a dark cloud that you are shedding, clearing from your body. With each in-breath, you become more filled with energy and relaxation, and with every exhalation, you rid your body of tension and negativity. As you continue to draw in light and energy with each breath, begin to visualize now that tiny white roots are growing down from your sit bones, down through the chair or the floor, down through the basement, down through layers of wood and concrete, reaching down now into the deep, rich earth that is the source of all life. See your roots spiraling down now into that sweet, dark richness and beginning to draw up earth energy, earth power being drawn up now through your roots, into your sit bones, all the way up your spine, earth energy moving up your spine now, filling your body with power and light, energy reaching upward and upward until it spills in a shower of light out through the top of your head, energy arching now like willow branches back to the earth again, energy going down into the dark, powerful earth. You are the center of a beautiful circle of light. You draw the energy up through your roots, up through your body, your body filling with light, energy pouring out through the top of your head, arching down to the earth. A bright circle of light and energy—and you are the center. Take a deep breath and open your eyes.

In addition to using ritual and guided meditation, another way to bring yourself into immediate alignment with the Tarot and with the inner self is to enlist the help of herbal allies. It is practically unthinkable for us to play Circle Games without a hefty mug of mugwort tea! Mugwort, a hardy weed that thrives just about anywhere you plant it, has been the Tarot herb of choice for centuries. Actually, mugwort is great for all types of divination, as well as for dream-work, but it works especially well with the cards. You can burn it as incense, either alone or in combination with other materials (cinnamon or sandalwood, for example). You can store your cards with some of it. And you can make a potful of tea with the dried herb. We use about a half cup of mugwort to six cups of boiling water and let it steep *at least* fifteen minutes. Mugwort is a relaxant that helps us to let go of our daily tensions, unwind, and focus on the cards. We have never heard of an adverse reaction to mugwort, but, as with any substance, its use should be carried out with caution and respect. Most people find that the taste grows on them: We buy it in bulk.

The Right Deck

Circle Games will work with just about any Tarot deck, provided it is completely pictorial (meaning that there are actual scenes created for every card, not just a picture of four wands, for instance, for the Four of Wands). But finding the right deck means a lot more than just buying the first deck you see at the local book shop or game store. To work for you, a deck must speak directly to your inner self. The images, the colors, the very tone of the deck must be both deeply familiar and yet filled with wonder and magick. If a deck is terrifically appealing to you, looks beautiful to you, chances are it will be the right one. But you may have to look at quite a few decks before you find it. You can reap a lot of frustration from trying to work with the *wrong* deck: If you find yourself staring at your cards and seeing nothing, don't blame yourself—get a new deck!

If you have a book shop or game store near you that will let you examine the decks they offer for sale—if they have display copies of each set—then you can't go wrong. We have bought several decks sight unseen, seduced by descriptions read in catalogs, only to be sadly let down. An actual visual check is the best insurance against disappointment. For some ideas about the decks available, see the Tarot Resources at the end of this book.

About Shuffling

The reason we shuffle or mix the cards is to place our personal energies into the deck. Shuffling is a magickal activity: It stills and focuses the self, and it allows the cards to arrange themselves in the pattern that we need to see.

We have noticed that people have more anxiety about shuffling than about any other aspect of the cards. Because most decks are considerably larger than ordinary playing cards (some decks, like the Motherpeace, are even round), the typical poker-player's shuffle is difficult and frustrating to achieve. So try our favorite method: Place the deck face down in a big pile on the table or the floor and stir them around with both hands as if you were stirring a big pot of soup. This tactile, soothing approach to mixing the cards is both relaxing and effective.

Another dilemma is knowing when to stop. One of the most-asked questions is, "How can you tell when you've shuffled enough?" For some of us, the answer is the same as the one our mothers gave us when we asked, "How will I know when I'm really in love?" You'll just *know!* If that answer doesn't help you, try another of our favorite methods: Sing a song, either aloud or in your mind's voice. When the song is done, so is the shuffling. This works especially well with groups—the sound of everyone singing together takes the self right out of ordinary reality and into magickal time, and it starts the process of group bonding immediately.

A Final Helpful Hint

There are times when a card just sits there and does not speak to you at all. This can be frustrating, particularly if you are attached to meanings and can't find one. One technique we have found to be helpful at times like these (and we all have them) is to try the Describe Me game. Pick up the troublesome card and look at it. Now simply describe, out loud, what the picture shows. Don't worry about what it means; just describe, in as much detail as possible, what is going on in the picture—colors, activities, people and their clothing, any animals or objects you see. Every detail is important. You never see the same card the same way from reading to reading. The court cards, especially, can change character radically. You will probably find that as you describe the card you will be describing your situation or issue perfectly. So simple: What you see is what it is.

So—come and join the circle. Happy playing!

Chapter 2

Games for a Small Circle

We begin with a circle—the round egg that encompasses the seed and then begins to divide and divide; the circle of the womb that nurtures and protects us as we grow; then the circle of light that we see for the first time as we birth ourselves. For many of us, there is a deep need to recover the inner stillness and wholeness, the safety and dark sweetness of the womb-of-all-possibility—the place where our deep self is respected and heard. Pressed by the demands of job and home and the perpetual command to produce, our inner voice often goes unheeded, drowned out by the din of our relentlessly busy outer lives. The inner voice is our own shining knowledge, a connection with and gift from the Great Mother. It has always been there, growing with us as we grew, waiting to be heard and shared.

The Circle Games that begin this book give us a safe place, a place to feel nurtured and strengthened, a chance for our wise self to come out and play, and to be clearly heard. As we play the games, our inner voice becomes stronger and more certain. And as we begin to feel at home in the landscape of the cards, as we recognize the truth of the patterns that emerge for us, we find that the Tarot gives us a magickal vocabulary to express our own inner wisdom.

The first games in this chapter are similar to traditional spreads or layouts—you can play them alone, in a quiet space (or in a bustling diner or cafe, for that matter), or you can play them in a circle of people who are invited to give you helpful, loving feedback and to share their insights with you. The games for one person are designed to help you approach change or challenge in your life in a safe space and in a playful spirit. Both nurturing and empowering, these games prepare the way for the new concept of Tarot games played interactively. After all, it often takes some inner work, which we need to do alone, before we can begin to reach out beyond ourselves.

Next, we offer games for couples. These are gentle and nonthreatening ways for two people to share their inner selves, to come to a better understanding of each other, and even to get real information to help resolve issues or differences. Some of the couples games could be regarded as "couples therapy," but here the partners are invited to consult their own inner wisdom rather than a therapist. The games are not limited to play between two people immersed in a romantic relationship; friends will enjoy the warmth of growing closer, too.

This chapter ends with games that can be played with one to three players—a fairly loose grouping that leads into chapter 3, "Games for a Larger Circle." You'll notice that many of the games cross the boundaries that we have assigned. The games are meant to be used in *any* way that seems right to you. Use the groupings as broad guidelines rather than as absolutes. If you want to play the children's game Autumn Leaves and there's not a kid in sight—go ahead! This book is all about strengthening the power of your inner knowing—and encouraging your sense of play—in community with others. Trust your own inner voice.

Magic Wand

This is a wonderful game to play if you need to check your empowerment level. The suit of Wands relates to fire, drive, the power that comes from inner conviction. If you have been feeling lethargic, or you can't seem to get out of your own way, Magic Wand can show you where your energy is blocked and give you some ideas on how to recover your drive.

Like other games in this book that are similar to more traditional spreads, Magic Wand can be played by several players together or in turn, each person finding her Magic Wand and the other players giving feedback and insights.

The Play

Mix the cards, allowing them to absorb your personal energy. Place the deck face down in front of you and begin to turn over the cards, one at a time, until you find a Wand card. If you get a Wand within the first five cards, then your sense of personal power is strong and manifesting without significant blocks at this time. The Magic Wand card that appears can show you where you feel strongest. The preceding cards give information on your sources of empowerment and the ways you manifest it in the world.

If you turn over more than five cards before finding your Magic Wand, then look at the preceding cards to find insights about possible energy blocks, or for areas that need special attention.

If you are feeling unsure of your direction, Magic Wand may help you to determine the steps you need to take to regain your wholehearted power and will. If you play it in the company of good friends who know the circumstances of your life, they may give you helpful interpretations of the cards that you might not have seen immediately. And it's good to remember that your choices—how you use your Magic Wand—are yours alone. All of us are magic wands, in the sense that we are channels for power and energy to be used for the good of all.

The Snake

The snake is an ancient and revered symbol of healing and regeneration. This game spread is ideal for those times when you feel itchy in your skin, ready to peel off and begin again. If you are at a turning point, Snake can help to guide the way by giving you information about your way of approaching things.

So if you need a change or you are thinking of starting something new, try playing Snake—she will affirm your path of personal evolution.

The Play

Mix the cards, sending your personal energy and openness into the deck. Then choose five cards at random and lay them out in the following pattern:

Card 1: Beginning—my usual approach, or one that would be helpful to me now

Card 2: What I carry—my baggage or challenge

Card 3: At my center

Card 4: Motivating force—what propels me forward

Card 5: What I leave behind

Pay special attention to the relationship between card 1 and card 2: One often brings clarity to the meaning of the other. Reversed cards are also significant in this game: They are often indications of issues that need to be dealt with before you can progress.

Cosmic Match

Sometimes you have five minutes to yourself, unexpectedly, and in that precious time you could massage your feet, or skim the headlines, or eat a piece of fruit, or—play Cosmic Match! Turning the cards over, one by one, until you find the single card that carries the message for you in this particular time and space can raise your cosmic consciousness. The card's message may be one of affirmation—you are in harmony with your inner self, your power is strong and accessible—or it may be one of instruction, of changes that need to be made. While it is hard to confine the wisdom of the Tarot to a single image, the card will offer some insight into the state of your life at this moment. The magickal fun of playing this game comes from the anticipation of *which* image—among the entire deck—will be your cosmic match.

The Play

Mix the cards until you have touched each one, putting your energy into the deck. It can help to repeat, inside yourself, something like, "I am here and ready to listen. . . ." Then stack the cards into a deck. Turn over one card at a time from the deck as you call out in sequence, either aloud or with your inside voice, the cards of the Minor Arcana (Ace, 2, 3, 4, 5, 6, 7, 8, 9, 10, Page, Knight, Queen, King), until the card that you have turned over matches the number or court card that you have just called out. Do not specify the suit but call out the number only.

If you don't have a Cosmic Match on the first sequence, start the sequence again with Ace and continue through the deck until a card matches; it may take two or three sequences. (It is nearly impossible to go through the entire deck without a match, but if that happens, reshuffle and *concentrate* your energies again.) If the number you call out matches the number of one of the Major Arcana, you are especially in tune with the universe today!

Sacred Cave

There are times when we need to retreat from our hectic schedules and find a safe place deep inside ourselves where we can curl up and be nurtured. Sacred Cave gives us such a place and forges a strong bond between ourselves and our cave-dwelling ancestors, who left their red handprints as legacies on the walls. Cave images hold rich significance for us, reminding us of safety, community, and the strong magick made by priestesses who danced and sang there. Caves are the wombs of Mother Earth. Any time you need to feel the arms of the Mother wrapped around you, you can play Sacred Cave. The Tarot will show you how to give yourself the nurturing you need.

The Play

Mix the cards face down and choose six cards at random. Arrange them in the pattern shown to form your own Sacred Cave. Although all the cards in your Cave are valuable allies, card 4 deserves special attention. It will help you to feel safe and protected.

Card 1: Where I am now
Card 2: Empowers me
Card 3: Keeps me company
Card 4: Shelters me
Card 5: What I seek here
Card 6: What I feel the need to create

Groups can also play Sacred Cave, either making neighboring caves and sharing the results or taking turns choosing cards to construct a single, communal cave. The cave may become a metaphor for the group itself. What importance does the group have for you? Why are you a part of it? What role does it play in your life? The cards may shed light on these questions for you.

Two or three friends can build a cave with thick walls, each player choosing a card for each position simultaneously from the pile. After the cave is constructed, the players can share their insights and interpretations with one another, opening the way for discussion.

For example, in the card position number 1 (where I am now), the Four of Wands and the Ten of Swords were chosen by two friends playing this game together, using the Morgan-Greer deck. The first player saw the Four of Wands, with its festival banner of flowers, as her optimistic approach to life. The other player agreed, but she also pointed out that this card could pertain to a project that her friend was rushing headlong to finish, more concerned with getting to the celebration at the end than with the process of completing the necessary work. The player who drew the Ten of Swords, which shows a figure pinned to the ground by bloody swords, thought that the card depicted the painful but necessary grieving process involved in giving up a creative project that was no longer viable but still much on her mind. Her friend pointed out that the card was also an affirmation: One meaning of the Ten of Swords is letting go of disappointment and accepting sacrifice in order to find your true path in life. Playing this game together gave both friends a sense of being supported, understood, and protected.

Five Seasons

The game we call Five Seasons is a gentle reminder of our likeness to the Earth. Like her, we have the seasonal ability to shift and change, grow and be still, each pattern gradually growing out of the last and into the next, a graceful circle dance that leads us to greater self-knowledge and greater respect for our planet. In this game, the fifth card gives us a season all our own, a season that reflects our inner being at the moment.

A simple, five-card game that can be played in a short amount of time, Five Seasons is a powerful key to understanding our rhythms, our times of stillness and waiting, our times of rebirth and activity. If you want more detailed information of a similar kind, you can play the Wheel of Life game, also included in this chapter.

The Play

Mix the cards, face down, and choose the following cards at random. Place these cards in whatever pattern feels most healing and hopeful to you.

Card 1: Summer—fruition, zenith
Card 2: Autumn—harvest, taking stock, letting go
Card 3: Winter—stillness, looking within
Card 4: Spring—renewal, hope, growth
Card 5: Season of the inner self—take this to heart and know that every season shifts and changes

Here are the Five Seasons that one woman, a healer and artist, chose: They gave her a gentle reminder of her issues and what to do about them. She chose the Motherpeace deck for this game, since the shape of these round cards echoes the wheel of the year.

Card 1, Summer: Two of Cups—this card shows the union of two figures, one dark and one light, each holding cups of the opposite color, creating a yin-yang effect. Dolphins play in the background. With its meaning of connecting polarities, playful harmony, and union, the player immediately thought of her ongoing work with a polarity therapist, who balances the energies of the body, and the creativity that is beginning to manifest as her inner work progresses. She also recognized the basically playful (and sexual) nature of her art.

Card 2, Autumn: Magician reversed—she saw in this the need to let go of a recurring fear of her own power. Often afraid to speak out, to take a stand, to make magickal change for the things in which she believes, she recognized this as her greatest block.

Card 3, Winter: Sun—this was a reminder that the winter months are her most creative. Rather than sink into depression, she needed to connect with others and use the dark time creatively, to make her own light, both alone and in community.

Card 4, Spring: Three of Cups—with its three ecstatically dancing figures, this card evoked the shared celebration of Full Moon circles, which are a Spring-like source of inspiration and joy for her.

Card 5, Inner Self: Eight of Cups—this card shows an octopus holding deep-sea treasures in each tentacle. She realized that her deep feelings, while sometimes overwhelming, offer great gifts—greater self-knowledge and creative inspiration.

Iris

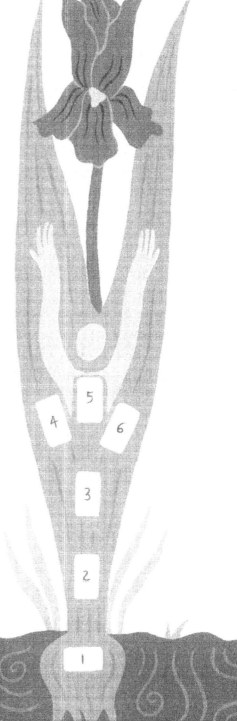

Based on the natural cycle of bulb or seed, sprout, leaf, and flower, Iris is useful when you are considering a new project or course of action.

Irises are associated with the subconscious and appear in several cards—for instance, you will find them glowing behind the Temperance angel in both the Rider-Waite and the Morgan-Greer decks. A tall stalk with graceful blooms, the mysterious and beautiful iris grows each year from its bulb deep in the earth, where it has wintered in darkness. What warming of the soil above signals new life? What, within us, will stir a new creation?

The Play

Mix the cards, face down, and then choose six cards at random. Lay them out in the following pattern:

Card 1: Seed—the beginning or inception. Placed sideways, this card may be read upright or reversed.

Card 2: Sprout—first stirrings. This card often gives useful information on the proper nurturing of the idea or project.

Card 3: Leaf and Stem—what is needed in order to grow and expand.

Cards 4, 5, 6: Flower—what can be expected to manifest. Look closely at cards 2 and 3 if what you see here is not what you had hoped for.

Besides being a wonderful game for one, Iris is also revealing when two people play it together. Curious about the outcome of a joint venture, two partners took turns pulling the cards, using the Morgan-Greer deck. Here are their readings.

Card 1, Seed: Seven of Pentacles—a figure stands in a field surrounded by ripening pentacles. Both players felt this was a good sign: They had done some solid preliminary work and could wait patiently, assured of a positive outcome.

Card 2, Sprout: The World—indicating cosmic consciousness, this card was a signpost. Rather than focusing on material concerns, they needed to concentrate on a higher purpose in the work they did together.

Card 3, Leaf and Stem: Eight of Swords reversed—this card had appeared over and over, in the upright position, in many readings for one of the partners. Both players took its reversal here to be a sign that constrictions and tensions were beginning to ease and that the joint project would benefit as a result.

Cards 4, 5, and 6, Flower: Emperor reversed—borrowing the Motherpeace interpretation for this card, both felt it indicated owning their own power and authority, as well as letting go of the need to control. Knight of Wands reversed—one player felt this warned against burnout, doing too much. The other player felt it concerned setting boundaries to protect her work time. High Priestess—a powerful image of the mysterious, hidden face of the Goddess, this card was exciting evidence that Her forces were blossoming in their project.

Deep Water

Deep Water focuses on the cards in the suit of Cups as keys to the feeling self.

All of us have times when we feel as if we are in deep water indeed, when feelings rise up like floodwater, threatening to overwhelm and engulf us. Then again, sometimes the waves of emotion can feel cleansing or liberating, washing over us harmlessly or picking us up and carrying us forward on a joyful tidal wave.

Being in right relationship with your feelings means, first, being in touch with them (it can be hard to deal with feelings if you are not really sure what they are). And second, it means being comfortable with them once they are clear. Deep Water can help you do both.

If you need a handle on your emotions, or if you want to feel more at home with your own feeling self, take a few minutes with your cards to dive into the warm and healing waters of this game.

The Play

Look at each card in the deck until you find one that sums up, as closely as possible, what you feel at the present time. If you can't do this, pick a card at random to depict this for you. Once the card is chosen, place all the other cards face down in a central pile—this is the pool of deep water—and let your card sink to the bottom of it by placing it face down beneath the others.

Now stir the cards with both hands. If you are playing this game with others, they can use a rainstick or make splashing sounds or hum "Deep River" while you do this—it's often good for us to let go of our seriousness when we approach our feeling issues.

Now close your eyes and dive into the pool by plunging your hands into the cards and taking out a handful. Open your eyes and look for Cups in the cards you have chosen. These are your guides. Look to them for information about your feelings and how they can best be healed or understood. See the gentle images of the Cup cards as keys to your own self-understanding. Trust your initial feeling about the cards, even if it doesn't conform to the "standard" meanings. For instance, if you draw the Motherpeace Ace of Cups, you may see the figure as fearing to dive into the water, unsure of the ability to breathe in such depths—even though the interpretation given in the accompanying book involves joyful surrender to the emotions. The truth is somewhere in between: Your vision is true for you for now and may indicate fear of deep commitment to a relationship, but the given meaning may point the way for you to take a deep breath and plunge in.

If you also brought up your original chosen card, then the message of the Cup cards is especially important to you at this time. If you did not bring up any Cups, you can try again—or you can feel comforted, knowing that your feelings are being bathed in the pool of Tarot wisdom.

If you want to take the game a step further, pick a card to represent any troubled or negative feelings that you would like to heal. Make a river of the cards by placing them face down in a wide line. Now send your chosen card "down the river" by placing it face down underneath the river of cards and gently pushing them away from you. Close your eyes and pick a card from the river to give you guidance. If you pick a Cup card, drink deep.

The Lovers' Game

The Tarot cards are wonderful allies for couples. The Lovers' Game creates a cozy and secure atmosphere in which to share your feelings and hopes as they are envisioned by the cards. After all, the true nature of intimacy involves opening up your inner self to another. This game is a key for doing just that—and it will lead you to an even deeper and more fulfilling relationship.

Just keep in mind that both partners need to approach this game in a spirit of loving cooperation and trust. This is not the place to grind your axes but rather to explore the closeness of mutual revelation.

The Play

After mixing the cards, each player picks six cards at random. You may simply play the cards in the order chosen, or you may decide which cards in your hand best fit the descriptions below.

Cards may be played simultaneously or in turn. Share what you see in the cards. And don't be afraid to take time with this game: With love and laughter, it may take all afternoon to share the wisdom of your special twelve cards.

Card 1: A relationship in the past that affects my present
Card 2: How I feel about your first card (place this card on top of your partner's first card)
Card 3: How our relationship affects me now
Card 4: Our strengths as a couple, as I see them
Card 5: How I feel this relationship is changing, or how it is changing me
Card 6: What I hope for in this relationship, and where I would like to see it go

The cards will reveal information about you and your partner that is intensely personal and specific to your own relationship. As you play the hand that is dealt to you, trust that the cards you hold are magickal windows on your life together. The cards will show you how your relationship with this particular partner has been affected by the past and changed by the present. It will also give you an idea of your shared hopes for the future. If there is trouble in paradise, feel confident: Your cards will give information on how to solve your problems together.

Here is an example of how one couple played the game. For the first card (a relationship in the past that affects the present), one partner put down the Lovers, a reminder of a passionate relationship in the past that had ended amicably and was not a threat to the present partner. Her partner put down the Seven of Swords, which shows a figure carrying shadow swords, a visualization of feelings associated with a painful divorce.

For the second card (how I feel about your first card), the first player put down the Five of Cups, a reminder not to dwell on loss and negativity but to embrace new love. Her partner played the Four of Cups, affirming that there are always choices of the heart, and that some people are lucky enough to love and be loved by more than one partner in their lives.

For the third card (how our relationship affects me now), the first player put down Judgment, a sign of the inner liberation that the relationship had already brought. Her partner played the Ace of Cups, a celebration of the joy of new beginnings.

For card four (our strengths as a couple, as I see them), the first player put down the Two of Wands, which is a clear image of partnership leading to vitality and shared energy. Her partner played the Page of Cups, enjoying the picture of playful humor and emotional spontaneity.

For card five (how I feel this relationship is changing), the first player's choice of the Queen of Cups revealed her joy in assuming her full power as a creative lover. Her partner played the Wheel of Fortune, honoring their ability to find the still center of their love amid ups and downs.

The last cards left in their hands (what I hope for in this relationship) were the Knight of Wands and the Page of Swords. Together, they made a remarkable picture of an energetic partnership with an exciting future.

Not all cards will be as clearly positive as the game depicted above—it really depends on the state of the players' relationship. Remember that the point of the game is to open loving discussion that leads to greater understanding of the self and each other. The Five of Pentacles drawn as the third card, for example, could point to a need for compassion and nurturing. The player who draws this card may need extra reassurance from the other.

Completion

In any relationship, there is a constant flow of give-and-take that leads to greater understanding, the resolution of issues, completion. This game visualizes that process. With a shared sense of fun, Completion shows couples how their energies combine for the good of both.

The Play

After mixing the deck face down, both players choose four cards at random. Each player holds her cards, facing toward her. Then they each take turns picking a single card at random from the other's hand. If a player picks a card that matches one of her own (suits match, numbers match, as do Major Arcana—for example, a Four of Cups would match a Six of Cups, and a Queen of Swords would match a Queen of Wands), then the player places the matched cards down on the table and opens a discussion about the feelings or issues depicted. You might begin by looking at the suits and their significance (Swords indicating the mental/intellectual realm, for example) and then see how the images relate to your shared life experience. Players continue doing this until one person plays her or his last card, or until there are no more matches possible. Any remaining cards can be shared as issues still in process.

Feelings and Needs

This game for two players is ideal not only for lovers/partners but for friends, relatives, co-workers—anyone who is in a relationship. A valuable ally to identify and heal sensitive areas between you, Feelings and Needs offers a gentle and nonthreatening way for people to communicate. And just sharing the enjoyment of playing together goes a long way toward building stronger bonds of closeness.

The Play

Players mix the cards and choose four cards each at random. You may play them in the order chosen, or you may pick the cards from your hand that best fit the descriptions below.

Players take turns putting down one card at a time and sharing their perceptions. Feedback from your partner is a vital part of the game.

Card 1: What I'm feeling right now
Card 2: What I have to offer
Card 3: What I need from you now
Card 4: What we need to examine closely

For the finale, both players pick a wild card from the deck to share. This is often a helpful hint that will give further insight on the fourth card.

Balance

So much of life is focused on striving for balance—or on maintaining it once we've achieved it or on coping with feeling out of balance when we haven't. Nowhere is this more keenly felt than in relationships, where people learn to deal not only with their own issues around balancing but also with those of their friends, partners, and lovers.

This game gently explores ways toward a better sense of balance, both as an individual and as a couple. Although it was originally intended as a two-player game, groups may also find it a valuable way to gain perspective and information.

The Play

Players mix the cards face down and then choose four cards each. Now turn the cards face up and examine them. Look at the cards numerically: Is one person carrying higher numbers, or are they evenly matched? Look at the suits: Do you see many of one suit in one hand or an even distribution?

Gently discuss the significance of your findings. Which areas need balancing? Many Cups, for instance, may indicate a need for emotional work, while many Wands may relate to issues of assertiveness or anger. Use your inner wisdom. Does one person feel she carries more responsibility for the relationship emotionally? Many high-number Cups may appear in her hand if so. Many Pentacles may indicate financial burdens or concerns that affect the players. Or, one of you may be at a crossroads—many Major Arcana in one hand may point out a time of great importance for the individual.

There are specific ways you can help each other to address any imbalance that comes up in the cards. For example, if you have a majority of Sword cards (which may indicate overintellectualizing or living too much in the head), and you realize that you are out of touch with your body, perhaps a foot massage from your partner will help you feel more grounded.

Give loving support to each other as you explore your balancing issues.

Family Portrait

This game is intended to give players a way to approach family issues in a gentle and healing way. Are you or your friends dealing with the pain of growing up in a "normal" American family? Is "dysfunctional" more than just a word for you? There just aren't many of us who have had stable, happy, and secure childhoods, and Family Portrait gives us a way to put our family experiences in perspective. It can be played with any number of people.

Do use your judgment: If addiction or abuse was part of your family's picture, some of the issues that this game will bring up may be too volatile to handle without the help of a counselor or therapist. But if you keep this in mind, the game will further your healing process and lead you to deeper understanding of your family's patterns.

Before you begin play, invoking some form of spiritual protection might help to make you feel safe and supported.

The Play

All players mix the cards, face down, and then each chooses five cards at random. Examine your hand: If you chose a court card, put it down on the table. Does it remind you of anyone in your family? Or the child that you were? Or the way you relate to your family now? The court card you chose represents a key person or attitude in your life, and the other cards in your hand will amplify your feelings about this card. Look for a healing card (the Star, for example, with its message of deserving blessings in your life) if healing is needed in this situation.

Players take turns putting their court cards down and looking for the perspectives and patterns that are suggested. If you did not choose a court card, keep choosing cards from the pile until you do. This is an indication that family issues are not central to your life right now. When you do find your court card or cards, the other cards in your hand will relate to the ones chosen.

You may play several rounds, dealing five cards each time. Family issues are rarely simple: Don't be surprised if the same family member makes several appearances in different aspects. The Queen of Cups, for example, could be the loving and nurturing mother, while the Queen of Pentacles reversed, showing up in the second round, could be the negative side of the same mother, overly involved with superficial, material concerns.

Playing this game in a circle of close friends may allow each person to support and encourage the others in their efforts to heal the past and embrace the present, where we are all free to create our own families.

Fish

This quick-and-easy game is deceptively simple. Fish packs a lot of information into a small package, making Tarot wisdom accessible even to those of us who "never have time."

Fish can be played alone or with others, and it offers an at-a-glance reality check. In group play, every player can draw from a central deck, or each player may use an individual deck.

Enjoy.

The Play

Mix the cards and choose three at random, placing them face up in a line.

Card 1: Worm, what I have to offer the universe at this time
Card 2: What I catch from the cosmic pool
Card 3: What I'll make of it

Wheel of Life

This game is based on the ancient circle of the seasons as they were celebrated by our ancestors. We call these holy days by their old names here, and we look to the beautiful pattern of our solar year when we need advice about our own cycles and seasons, our times of waiting and renewal.

Like Sacred Cave, this game is primarily intended for solitary play, but it can be enjoyed by groups of up to eight players, each person becoming a spoke of the wheel, taking turns choosing a card.

The Play

Sit in the center of the floor. Mix the cards, face down, and then choose eight cards and put them in a circle around you, in the pattern shown below. Notice how the cards balance each other. Look at what is behind you and before you. Turn slowly and savor the feeling of being part of the circle.

Card 1 (Yule): Winter Solstice, when the longest night of the year gives way at dawn to the rebirth of the sun. Renewal.

Card 2 (Imbolc): The seeds begin to waken beneath the earth. Planting ideas.

Card 3 (Ostara): Spring Equinox, when day and night are in balance. Egg-time: Growth.

Card 4 (Beltane): Celebration of fertility and sexuality.

Card 5 (Litha): Summer Solstice, the longest day of the year. Brightness.

Card 6 (Lughnasad): Celebration of the grain. First fruits.

Card 7 (Mabon): Autumn Equinox, day and night in balance. Harvest.

Card 8 (Samhain): Traditional day for divination and honoring our ancestors. Looking within.

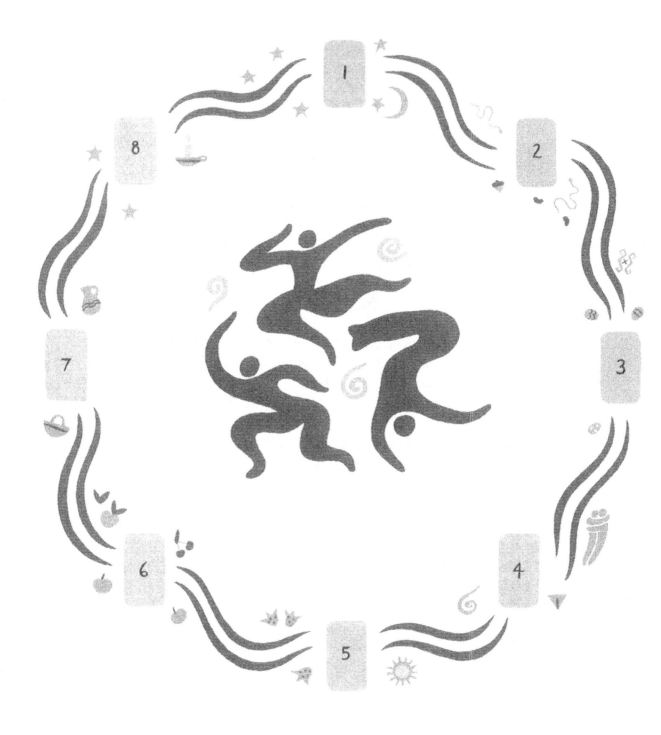

Look at the cards you have drawn as they relate to your own sense of ebb and flow. If you feel stuck, the Yule card brings hope or identifies areas of blockage to be freed up so that light can return to your life. Imbolc gives us information on beginnings: What ideas or projects are stirring for you? The Ostara card shows your pattern of growth. Are there weeds in your life? What will you choose to nurture? The Beltane card gives perspective about your sexuality at this time. Litha shows you how to shine. What do you need to do in order to share your gift with others? The Lughnasad card can tell you what you have been reaping lately, or what you need to concentrate on in order to bring something to fruition. Your Mabon card focuses on giving thanks. What are you grateful for? What do you need to shed in order to embrace thankfulness? And the Samhain card encourages us to deepen, letting go of the need for activity, stilling the self so that we can hear the inner voice.

There is a connection between your life and the circle of the year. Celebrate your unique place in the circle.

Birthday Game

As we get older, we need *more* celebration and magick around our birthdays rather than less! The Birthday Game is a way for adults to rediscover the joyful expectation and delight that children feel at their solar return. The next time you turn a year older, do something really nice for your own inner child and play this game.

The Play

As you mix the deck, focus on the events of your life and your hopes for the future.

Now make a round, cake-shaped pile by placing one card face down for every year of your age—and one to grow on. There are seventy-eight cards in the deck, so if you're seventy-seven years old or older, congratulate yourself on your elder status and use the entire deck.

Hold your hands over the cake and make a wish. Now blow on the cake—and turn one card face up. Either your wish may be granted immediately or the card will tell you what you need to resolve in order for the wish to materialize. (Wishing for a promotion? Maybe you'll pick the Three of Wands, which shows someone assured of success, wealth, and power.)

Happy Birthday.

Tea Party

This game can be very liberating and a lot of fun: Break the stereotype of the sedate tea party and let the spirit of the Mad Hatter and friends enter into your group.

The Play

One player "pours" by placing two cards in front of each player: the first face up (the saucer) and the second face down on top (the teacup). Each player lifts the teacup card and looks at it: This is the card you need to "drink," or absorb, so take a moment to see how it makes you feel. If you were "poured" a Cup card, the significance is very great for you at this time. Now look at the saucer card beneath. This card will clarify and give support to the meaning of the first card and may indicate issues of importance at this time. One mother who played this game was poured the Temperance card atop the Tower reversed. With a wry grin, she confessed that her life was in turmoil because her young child had been engaging in violent temper tantrums—fortunately, the destruction was minimal—but she was heartened by the promise of healing and harmony held out by the angel in the teacup card.

If you want to take the game a step further, you can "read the tea leaves" by spinning the cards face up on the floor and then looking at the colors and shapes of the cards rather than at the images. Do you notice any significant patterns? Try looking at the cards from unusual angles. Close one eye. Lie on your side. Anything goes! This different way of seeing can yield surprising results.

Prosperity

What a can of worms we open when we talk about money: our need for it, our collective societal obsession with it, our distrust of it (and sometimes of those people with lots of it). Many of us have some serious healing work to do around the whole money issue. This game can help.

The Prosperity game gives us useful information about the many levels of tangible reality, about the connections between bodily health, income, job/work, home—the entire material package. The game also shows us where we may have blocks and issues that keep us from creating the healthiest and most prosperous (in every sense) reality possible. When we begin to question the true nature both of our needs and of our sense of abundance, we begin to unlock the meaning of the Pentacle cards—and of our own relationship to material reality.

The Play

Mix the cards, face down, in a pile, and then each player chooses four cards at random. You may play the cards in the order chosen, or you may pick the cards in your hand that seem most appropriate to each description below. Pay special attention to any Pentacle cards; since it is the suit that corresponds to the material world, these cards are the keys to this game.

Card 1: The present state of my material reality
Card 2: The source of my deprivation—what makes me feel needy
Card 3: The source of my abundance—what makes me feel rich
Card 4: What I need to do or embody in order to find my own true prosperity

Working through this kind of information can be tremendously healing for all involved. As a final affirmation, you may each wish to choose a card that depicts abundance and well-being and place these in the center of the playing space for all to share: "Give-aways" are a gesture of faith in the universe.

Chapter 3

Games for a Larger Circle

So many of us are actively involved in creating a true community, one based not just on proximity but on a primal need for deep closeness and the support of like-minded people. Given a mutual desire for sharing, exploring, and affirming our true selves, people belonging to many different kinds of groups can benefit from the games in this section.

Games for a Larger Circle are designed to enhance group activity. They serve a variety of purposes: They help those who have just met to break the ice; they build group trust; they help individuals discover their strengths and their own unique places within the group. And, as with any Tarot activity, they enhance self-awareness and enable us to go beneath the superficial to something very meaningful and powerful indeed. As Starhawk cautions in *The Spiral Dance*, "When inner vision becomes a way of escaping contact with others, we are better off simply watching television. When 'expanded consciousness' does not deepen our bonds with people and with life, it is worse than useless: It is spiritual self-destruction." Games for a Larger Circle provide a context for strengthening bonds and for sharing our inner vision in a loving and deeply exciting way.

It is no accident that the group games are a lot of fun and encourage us to play and even be a little silly: There is no better way to strengthen connection than to allow our inner children to come out and play together.

If you are not already involved in a group, perhaps these games will inspire you to start one for the sole purpose of playing them! We can envision whole evenings centered around the games. Remember the bridge and poker parties our parents used to have? Remember the stress and competition that accompanied those activities? *These* card parties would be very different! Circle Games are a way for us to heal and encourage each other, empower ourselves, validate our process of change, and discover loving sisterhood and friendship based on real understanding.

Empress

The Empress card, a powerful depiction of the Goddess in her birthing/nurturing aspect, is an important image for women as we reclaim our sacredness as creators. Whether we choose to birth babies, or books, or lush and fruitful gardens—whatever channel our creative energies choose to take—the Empress can be our inspiration.

This game for groups is designed to affirm each player's power and remind you of your own Goddess-like ability to create, relate, and nurture.

The Play

After each player shuffles the cards, divide the cards into as many piles as there are participants. Examine the cards in your pile: If you get the Empress, you are Queen for the Day and may make wishes, plan projects, receive gifts—whatever your heart desires. Look at the other cards in your pile for ideas on what you would like to manifest in your life right now. If nothing appeals, other players may give you cards: The Motherpeace Six of Discs, which shows the giving and receiving of a nurturing massage, would be a welcome gift to someone under tons of stress, for example. Or you may "blue sky"—that is, tell your dreams, your fantasies—and everyone can share your hopes and make plans to turn them into realities. You may mix the cards and play again until everyone has a chance to be Empress, or, if the group is large and time too short, end the play when it feels right.

Seed Sowing

This game works best for interactive groups—not strangers, but people who have come together to work on specific tasks or issues, who know one another through group work, and who are open to using the information revealed by the cards to enhance their progress toward the group goals, whatever they may be. For focus groups or self-help groups, Seed Sowing can be used to open discussion of the concerns shared by all members. For groups on spiritual retreat, Seed Sowing can direct the energies of the participants toward meditation and inner knowing, together.

The Play

By consensus, the group consciously chooses a card from the deck that relates to the group as a whole—a card whose image is central to the present situation or issue under discussion. This card is placed face up in the middle of the floor. Each player mixes the deck, directing her personal energy into the cards. Then the deck is divided into as many piles as there are players and each player selects a pile.

Walking in a circle together (preferably in a clockwise direction), each player tosses a total of five cards toward the center—in a motion reminiscent of casting seeds onto a tilled field. Only those that fall face up are read. Some cards will fall on or near the central card: These are closest to the central concern and should be given special attention, particularly as they relate to the players who tossed them. Other cards will land farther away from the center and will be less important, but the information they contain will still be relevant to the group.

This simple game, by literally sowing the seeds of discussion, provides a wonderful opening for group interaction and interpretation.

©1993 DURGA

Gifts and Secrets

This game can be played with as few as two players, but it is even more fun with more. It is a great way for people to get to know one another better within the context of sharing insights—a fine and gentle way to explore together.

The Play

All players mix the cards face down, and then each person chooses four cards at random. The players take turns putting down their cards, one by one, in the following sequence:

Card 1: Select a card from your hand that says something about you that you would like the other players to know. Describe what the card signifies to you. (Other players may feel free to add interpretations if they wish.)

Card 2: Close your eyes and pick a card from your hand at random. Put it down in front of you and don't say a word about it yourself—let the other players tell you what they see.

Card 3: Choose a card from your hand that you would like to give as a gift to one of the other players and put it down in front of that person. Explain its significance.

Card 4: The last card in your hand may remain your secret, or you can put it down in front of you and share its information with the other players.

Gifts and Secrets remains one of the most popular games we have played with our friends and with students in our workshops. Playing it together affirms the commonality of experience we all share as fellow travelers on this planet.

Magic Carpet

If your group needs a nurturing recharge, this game will take you to a place where you can play, imagine, and refresh your inner self. Relaxation work or a short guided meditation may help set the stage for your trip.

The Play

 Everyone mixes the cards and places them face down, spread out enough so that they form the shape of a magic carpet on which all participants can sit. Close your eyes and choose one person to pick a card she is sitting on. She looks at it to discover the destination of the magic carpet ride.

Now the player closes her eyes again and describes the scenery depicted on the card. Everyone takes turns adding to the description: scents, bird calls, the sound of waves or wind in the trees—make this as detailed and real as possible. Imagine that you are there and how that feels. Share your impressions. Offer suggestions—what pleasant or exciting things could happen here? Will you meet anyone or anything that can help or inspire you? Take turns imagining the whole scenario. When the magic carpet ride has been fully enjoyed, return to ordinary reality: Take a deep breath and open your eyes.

Blind Faith

This game is about the power of surprise and trust. Sometimes it is not possible or even desirable to see everything laid out in front of you. Sometimes you just need to close your eyes and put your hands in the cosmic pool and grab—an act of faith—and the message that you need right now will surface. Blind Faith also gives us information about our connections to one another and the ways in which we are necessary to each other as we travel our paths.

The Play

Place the cards face down in a central pile and mix them. With eyes closed, everyone picks a card simultaneously. Open your eyes and examine the cards. If the universe has gifted you with two or more cards that match numerically or by suit, players celebrate these unexpected connections and share what they see. Nonmatching cards are mixed back into the pile. This can be played indefinitely or until a set number of matches has been made.

Symbol Seeker—
A Magickal Treasure Hunt

You can play this game with total strangers or longtime friends and the results are always illuminating. A wonderful way to deepen your understanding of the Tarot and of one another, Symbol Seeker will help you discover some fascinating connections between cards. The object of the game is to put all your cards on the table (literally and metaphorically!), but in order to do this, each player must look very carefully at the images depicted on the cards.

The Play

All players mix the cards face down, and then each person chooses three cards at random from the deck. If you have any Major Arcana, place them face up on the table and take turns sharing insights about their personal significance. Now for the fun and the challenge: Once all the Major Arcana have been played, players must examine the Minor Arcana in their hands to find objects or symbols on them that match symbols on the Major cards already showing. Here are some examples of matches using the Morgan-Greer deck. A flaming red, equal-armed cross figures prominently in the Judgment card, and the King of Rods has a similar equal-armed cross in gold, which holds his cloak in place. Both the High Priestess and the Empress have crescent moons beneath their feet—and the Eight of Cups has a crescent moon in the sky. The Justice card has a scale and so does the Six of Pentacles (although the Justice one is not balanced and the Pentacles one is). If you can find a symbol in your hand that matches a card on the table, place your card beside its match. Open group discussion on the ways that the cards are related—and how they relate to your lives. Players may then try to match symbols on the Minor Arcana that have been played. Ideally, everyone will be able to place all their cards down, and many insightful connections will be made.

Maiden, Mother, Crone

This game invokes the three phases of Woman/Goddess/Moon, an ancient and deeply magickal triad. Maiden, Mother, Crone offers insight, strength, and empowerment while affirming the connection that is every woman's birthright. The Motherpeace deck is an ideal choice for this game, since its imagery includes several Daughters and mothers, and it has a Crone instead of the traditional Hermit.

The Play

After mixing the cards face down, each player picks a card at random to represent the "Maiden" self. This may represent your actual childhood and how it shaped your present reality, or it may give information about the youthful, free, and unattached part of yourself. Share stories with one another.

Next, pick a card to represent the "Mother" part of the self. This may show how you nurture yourself and others, or how you manifest your creative power in the world.

Now pick a final card to represent the "Crone" self. Society being what it is, this card is likely to trigger some fear and negativity, but reclaiming the honor, strength, and power of our elder status is an important part of this game. What barriers do we need to overcome in order to embrace the Crone? What will we have to offer the world when we become the Crone ourselves? Celebrate the wonder and magick of our metamorphoses: Share and affirm the power of *all* our phases.

Acting It Out

This game is terrifically freeing and fun, a way of involving your body and the cards together to liberate and strengthen the self. We absorb knowledge not only with the mind but with the physical senses as well.

The Play

All players mix the cards face down, and make a pile in the center of the space. Close your eyes and pick one card from the pile. Now take turns acting out the card you have chosen. While the game may seem similar to mime work, this does not have to be a silent game at all—everyone is invited to talk and share feelings and insights.

Some examples show how the game works: During one game, a player drew the Eight of Swords, which depicts a bound and blindfolded figure surrounded by swords. In acting out this teaching card, the player focused on the dress that the figure wears—open at the heart as if torn—and acted out ripping her shirt open, feeling exposed and vulnerable, and tearing her hair. Acting out these uncomfortable feelings was a release, a very active way of dealing with the feelings of vulnerability and exposure that the player had been experiencing.

Another player drew the Chariot, which she liked but for which she didn't quite feel ready. As she tentatively began to mime getting the reins of her life in her hands—as she imagined the pull of the horses and the empowered feeling of the figure in the chariot—she began to actually embody the card. Really experiencing the Chariot card with her body invited that energy more fully into her life.

Sword Warrior

This active group game is all about the power of swords. To play Sword Warrior, it helps to think of swords as protective and enlightening, cutting away falsehood or foggy notions; they are not only hurtful weapons. The Sword cards give us insight about the intellect, our thoughts and minds. Although it is true that the mind can be a fascist, choking inner freedom with "shoulds" and "thou shalt nots," tangling itself up in elaborate schemes, losing sight of the heart's reality, the rational mind can also be a brave and valiant champion of the self.

Sword Warrior is a way to connect with the positive power of the Sword cards. When you play it, expect to feel both silly and empowered—and have fun.

The Play

Players sit in a circle around a central pile of cards, which they all mix together. Then each player chooses a card. If you draw a Sword card, stand up. When two or more players have Sword cards, challenge each other—hold your cards out at arm's length, like swords, and "duel" (gently) with them. This is not about winning or losing, but about healing our pain and owning our power: If you don't like your Sword card—if its image is one of the painful ones, like the Ten of Swords—allow the holder of a more positive Sword to heal yours by releasing it back into the central pile: Drop your card. If both players hold positive Swords, end the duel by saluting and acknowledging each other.

Swords of equal positive power can be used for the good of the group to protect and empower the participants: Place them face up around the outside of the circle. Players may continue to draw from the pile until everyone draws a Sword card or until no new Sword cards appear.

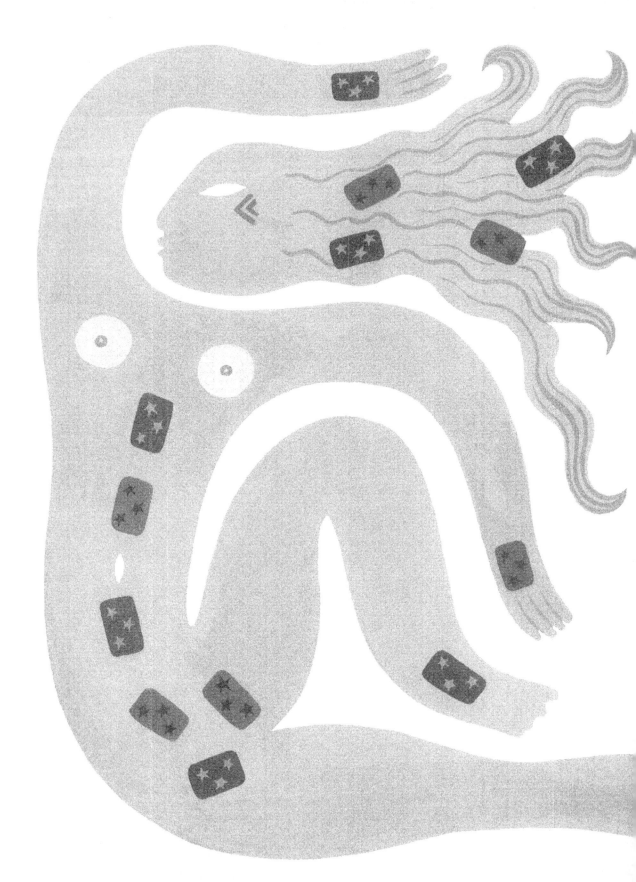

Body of the Goddess

The next time you feel depressed about your body, or angry at the Madison Avenue approach to the female form, play this game with your friends and remember: We are all incarnations of the Goddess and our bodies are not only beautiful—they are sacred.

The Play

Together, the players will use the cards to make an image of the Goddess. After mixing the cards, each player takes turns choosing a card and placing it on the floor or the table to represent a part of the Goddess's body, explaining what the card she has chosen says about that part and about her own feelings. For instance, one player may put the Ace of Swords down for the head, saying, "This Goddess has wonderful new ideas, and I love that inspired, clear feeling in my own mind." Then the next player may choose the Three of Cups and put it down for the heart, saying, "I want to keep joyful sharing with my women friends at the center of my heart." The next player may place the Queen of Pentacles down for one hand, saying, "I choose to create a beautiful garden with my own hands, knowing that I am the Queen of my material reality." Some cards may reflect negative or troubled feelings about certain areas: Compassionate sharing of these will be helpful and healing to all. Play continues until the Goddess feels complete: Make the shape as simple or as elaborate as you want. Take a moment at the end of play to celebrate your power and creativity. Know that *you* are Goddess.

Earth, Water, Fire, and Air

This game is based on an ancient concept that links the four elements, the four directions, and the four suits of the Tarot—all very powerful stuff. If you are feeling a need for safety and protection, this is a helpful game to play. More information on this ancient concept, called correspondences, can be found in the Further Reading section at the end of this book.

This game can be played alone, but we offer it here as a way for groups to align with the elemental/directional energies.

The Play

For this game you will need to have a rough idea of where north, south, east, and west are in relation to you and your space.

Sit on the floor and divide the deck into suits. Four different group members volunteer or are chosen by consensus to "call in" each direction. The north person chooses a card that attracts her from the suit of Pentacles and places it on the floor to the north. Look at it and feel the strength and power of the earth, your body, your material reality. The west person chooses a card from the suit of Cups and places it on the floor to the west. As you look at it, feel the power of water, of your own fluidity, of the tears and emotions that cleanse and renew. Next, the south person chooses a Wand and places it to the south. Feel the power of fire, of your own life-energy, passion, and drive. Finally, the east person chooses a Sword and places it to the east. As you look at it, feel the power of air, of the realm of thoughts and ideas, and the power of the mind. You have made a circle of power. Take a moment to visualize the balanced energies of the cards and of the elements protecting you in each direction.

Now every player chooses a card from each suit at random. Allow the cards to give you information about the areas of your life that need attention. Put these cards underneath the four direction cards and know that you will have help as you work on the issues at hand.

You may wish to thank the four directions/elements before gathering the cards together and opening the circle.

Mask

Masks are transformative: If you have never experienced the freedom and power of wearing a mask, try this game. With a little practice, your group will find the link between masks and a very real sense of magick.

Doing some relaxation or deepening work before beginning play may be helpful—but some groups will be able to jump right in, finding that the wisdom of the cards speaks through them effortlessly.

The Play

After mixing the cards face down, each player chooses a card at random. This is your mask. Look at it and absorb the feeling of the card. Now place it in front of your face and speak as if the figure or image in the card were speaking. You may direct your comments to one person or to the entire group. After each player has spoken as her or his mask, share your reactions and insights.

Comforter

This is one of the most nurturing and comforting activities a close-knit group can do together—and it's lots of fun. It feels great to laugh and be silly while the group gives warmth and affirmation. You will be surprised at the powerful feelings of love and caring that emerge in this simple game. Children will enjoy snuggling under the cards, too.

The Play

Each participant takes a turn lying on the floor. Other group members divide the deck into shares and mix their cards. Then players gently allow their cards to fall, one by one, onto the reclining player until she is covered by a comforter of cards. Players take special note of any cards that fall face up, pointing them out in a supportive and loving way to the one under the comforter.

Sun, Moon, Star

This wonderful group game can be used in several ways—to help make decisions, to give insights on specific issues or questions facing the group, or simply as a way of getting closer while having meaningful fun.

Individuals can also play Sun, Moon, Star by themselves, allowing these powerful cards of the Major Arcana to show the way to successful resolution of the issues at hand.

The Play

Players mix the cards. Then each player reaches into the central pile and takes a handful of cards. Players examine their cards to see if someone holds the Sun, the Moon, or the Star. Generally, the Sun card heralds positive, warm, and healing energy, growth, and leadership for the good of all. The Moon card shows powerful unconscious forces, a need for going within, for surrendering to the messages of dreams, and indicates intuitive gifts and transformation. The Star indicates spiritual blessings, radiance, and renewal. In what ways are these significant for the players who drew them, and how do they relate to the group?

Or, you can divide the cards into piles representing various issues under consideration. Which pile has the Moon card? Perhaps the solution to that issue will manifest in a dream, or the group could try a guided meditation to find the answer in the unconscious. The Sun issue may resolve itself quickly: Perhaps positive action is called for. The Star offers great spiritual insight—there may be a blessing here. One issue may involve more than one of the three cards.

Dreaming the Dark:
In Honor of Starhawk

When a body is placed in the earth, it is reduced to bare bones. Our own dreamtime, like the darkness of earth, gives information about our interior space, the structure of our inner selves, the bare bones of our existence. By honoring our dreams together, we affirm the importance of our inner processes and share our most authentic selves.

We named this game in honor of Starhawk, whose writings on Goddess-consciousness have inspired so many of our waking and sleeping dreams.

The Play

Make a pile of cards in the center of the group: This is the earth, the dark ground of dreamtime. Players mix the cards using both hands, stirring the cauldron, until the cards feel warm. Then each person chooses a card. This is the Dream Card—it can reflect an actual night dream, or it can give information about the inner, dreaming self. Each person then tells the dream aloud: Invent one around the card's image if you cannot recall an actual dream. One woman who played this game, inspired by choosing the Motherpeace Seven of Wands, which shows a figure standing tall in her priestess power even as she is challenged by others around her, told this dream: "I am naked and unafraid before a group of my peers. It is time for me to tell what I know. I am strong in my commitment. Even the anger and confrontation that face me are empowering. I raise my arms and channel great, healing energy for the good of all. I wake feeling fiery and unafraid."

Once all the dreams are told, each person then chooses a second card. After examining it, you may choose to give the card as a dream-gift to the player for whom you feel it will be most valuable. Or you may keep it yourself, explaining its significance in your life. For instance, a woman just entering midlife drew the Motherpeace Death card as her second card. She decided to keep it as a strong reminder of the snake who sheds her old skin when it has been outgrown and of her own powerful ability to make the changes needed to support her own growth.

After sharing dreams, visions, and stories, all players join hands around the pile of cards and breathe onto them, inspiring one another toward deeper dreams and insights to come.

Chapter 4

Games Especially (But Not Only) for Children

Why Tarot games for children? Because it's never too early to connect with your inner stuff. The images on the cards are powerful, riveting, and full of mystery—just the right elements to fire a young imagination. The games that we play with children allow them to tap into the psychic power embodied in those images; like the Magician, we can help our children learn to take the ancient wisdom expressed in the Tarot and apply it to the practical and spiritual challenges in their everyday lives. Just think how different the world would be if all people were encouraged from childhood to pay attention to their own inner wisdom. If children were shown how to empower themselves by trusting their inner voice, there would be a lot more adults who are happy and secure.

The Circle Games in this section are meaningful and heart-centered activities that you can share with children. Parents who want to nurture and encourage their kids by helping them understand themselves will find that these games offer real insight. In fact, there is really no better way to find out about your child than by exploring these games together. And besides, the games are *fun*—and they actively encourage children to think about their lives in a positive and empowered way.

Actually, these games aren't just for kids—grown-ups love playing them, too. Some of the adults we know name two or three of these as their all-time favorites. But if you find it difficult to relax and be childlike alone or in the company of other grown-ups, find a kid. The two of you can play these games together, both of you will learn something important, and you'll have a great time doing it.

Build a House

This game is a wonderful way to familiarize children with the cards. And it offers a fun and nonthreatening way for young ones to express how they feel about their family and their sense of home. You can learn a lot about a child by quietly observing this game.

The Play

First spread all the cards out, face up. The child then chooses eight cards that are especially appealing to her or him and uses these eight cards to outline the shape of a house on the table or the floor. Some children make conventional house shapes, others make yurts or teepees. More cards are chosen from the pile to be windows and a door. Then court cards are chosen to be the people living in the house and are placed beneath the window and door cards: When a window is "opened," a court card is looking out.

Encourage children to talk about these imaginary people—what they tell you can be very revealing, and the game becomes the starting place for creative storytelling and imaginative play.

Animal Friends

Children have a special affinity for the world of animals, evident in countless beloved bedtime stories and stuffed toys. Many Tarot decks are filled with animal friends of all types, and they provide a special point of reference for children, one with which they feel instantly comfortable and at home.

Animal Friends is perfect for very young children. Older children may want to try Guardian Angel, a more sophisticated game also based on the idea that there are helpful entities in the cards.

The Play

All players mix the cards, face down, and choose a card at random. If there is an animal shown on the card, all players act out that animal: Roaring lions, barking dogs, hissing snakes, crawling crabs, and other wonderful creatures will fill the room. Players continue choosing cards until each child has drawn an animal card.

Children may be encouraged to talk about the animal they drew, naming its special, helpful qualities and how these relate to her or his life.

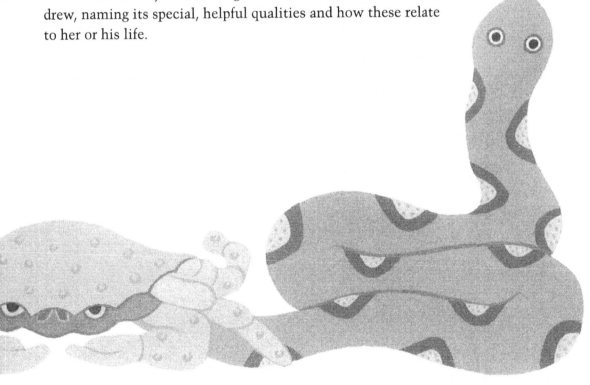

Autumn Leaves

We must never forget that children delight in the simplest of games. It's fun to cut leaf shapes out of paper and then stand on a chair and let them go. Children, fascinated, will watch them drift down for seemingly endless periods of time. (Try this with a roomful of relaxed adults and you'll get a similar response.) Hence this game, a salute to the beauty of autumn and its lessons on the grace of letting go.

The Play

The player mixes the cards and then stands on a chair and drops ten cards, one by one, from this height. Only the cards that fall face up are read. These may indicate attitudes or beliefs that the child is beginning to outgrow or needs to let go. Let the child tell you what she or he sees in the autumn "leaves."

Plant the Seed

Think about the daily miracle of a plant growing: How the seed stirs in the dark ground and sends a blind sprout up to the sun; the sprout becomes a green stalk with tender leaves uncurling slowly; and finally a flower unfolds.

Like Iris, this game focuses on the process of growth, but it involves younger players in a simpler and more active way. Learning how to nurture our own growth processes can begin at a very young age—and learning that our choices can make things flower is a valuable lesson that Plant the Seed can teach.

The Play

First choose a card to be the "seed," the beginning of something you would like to start or see happen. "Plant" this seed by placing it face down anywhere in the deck. Mix the cards and think about your seed growing. Then turn over the top card to see what will blossom. If you do not like what you see, turn over the next three cards to find out how to take care of your seed, to make sure your harvest will be a happy one. Or you can pick another seed and try again—remember that not every seed germinates, and sometimes starting over is the wisest thing to do.

Through the Door

Of all the Circle Games for children, this one seems to be everyone's favorite. It is an active game that will give a very clear picture of a child's natural abilities and will help her or him develop potential in a natural and joyous way. Through the Door is a valuable resource for adults who wish to obtain a specific sense of a child's talents and inclinations. And kids love to play it.

The Play

The player shuffles the cards and then picks two cards at random to be the door. These are placed face up about eighteen inches apart on the floor. The two cards often represent significant milestones in the child's development, or the next level through which

she or he must pass in order to grow and deepen.

The player sits about three feet away and tries to slide five cards, chosen at random, face down through the door. Examine the cards that make it through the doorway: These are indications of the child's natural gifts and talents. The Three of Cups, for example, points to the child's ability to sustain loving friendships, while the Three of Pentacles shows someone who can become a master at anything she or he practices. Cards that don't make it through the door are often the areas the child needs to work on in order to progress. The Three of Swords, which shows a heart pierced with swords, may indicate a sensitive child's need to avoid taking criticism too deeply to heart.

Loving and supportive discussion can be a valuable outgrowth of this game.

Wishing Well

There has always been something powerful about the act of throwing a coin in a wishing well. For centuries, people have done this in honor of the Goddess, throwing objects into her sacred pools and springs as offerings. This simple, magickal game can be played with any number of players and appeals to children of all ages.

The Play

Players make a wishing well by placing all the cards face down in a circle on the floor or the table. Each player chooses a card at random and, without looking at it, makes a wish and throws it down, aiming for the center of the well. If the card lands in the center, the wish has a great chance of coming true: Take a look to see what's in store. If you miss the center of the well, look at the card to see what issues need your attention in order for your wish to manifest.

Guardian Angel

Every child has fears and occasional bad dreams—part of the package of being so vulnerable and small. As parents, we strive not only to protect but to empower our children, and this game developed as way of doing just that. Children love this game because it reminds them that they have both inner resources and magickal allies—whether we call them totem animals, power objects, or guardian angels.

The Play

The player mixes the cards and chooses three at random. Look for positive figures or objects: These are important symbols for the child. For example, a large Pentacle image could be described as a magickal shield that keeps the child healthy and safe. Swords and magic Wands are very powerful, and Cups are filled with magic protection potions.

People shown on the cards can be valuable allies. Encourage the child to give them names and describe how they can help her or him to feel strong and safe. For example, the Knight of Cups can take a gentle, dreamy child with him to a quiet, beautiful place filled with music and peace. The Queen of Swords can teach an active child the art of self-defense with her sword, offering empowerment on a very real level. And the Temperance card in many decks is a graphic depiction of the guardian angel.

After the game is over, parents can remind the child of the images discovered in the cards. Encourage the child to draw or make the power objects or to tell stories about the magickal allies.

Circle of Protection

This one-player game, like the group game Earth, Water, Fire, and Air, gives protection and strength. Its simplicity makes it ideal for children, but adults enjoy it, too.

The Play

Seated on the floor, the player picks out ten of her favorite cards. It's not unusual for these to change from day to day, depending on what is going on in the player's life at the time.

Placing the cards face up in a circle around her, the player then closes her eyes and spins herself around several times. When she opens her eyes, she picks the first card she sees and looks at it. This is her strongest protection card for the day, and it gives information about what she needs in order to feel safe and loved.

Now the player turns slowly, with eyes open, taking a few moments to enjoy the security and happiness of being inside the circle of magickal cards.

Quest

Children love to be heroes—and they love the idea of going on special adventures. This game is a meaningful way for children to play out their empowering fantasies of brave deeds and special quests. And it can give them some real direction as they begin the adventure of their own lives.

The Play

The player mixes the cards face down. Then she turns the cards over one by one until she reaches a Knight. The Knight's suit shows what type of quest the child will undertake that day:

Wands: Energy, power. Get fired up about something and take steps to change things. Get angry about a real injustice and *do* something about it. Let your energy flow. Use the will.

Cups: Feeling, intuition, creativity. Write a poem or paint a picture. Tell a dream or a memory that brings up a lot of emotion. Let yourself feel sad for a bit, or abandon yourself to joy. Use the heart.

Pentacles: The physical or material. Comb or brush a pet, give someone a massage, knead bread, or go on a walk to find magickal objects in nature—a feather, a stone. Use the body.

Swords: A new idea or inspiration. Read a special book or solve a puzzle. Think something out, make lists, get it straight. Use the mind.

Pay special attention to the suit cards preceding the Knight. If three or more match the Knight's suit, this could be a general life-direction for the child, her natural way of relating to or perceiving the world.

Who Are You?

This game recognizes the importance of role models, who inspire our children toward a sense of their own unique human potential. The Tarot court cards, particularly as expressed in the Motherpeace deck, provide just such a set of role models. By consciously connecting with and affirming the value of role-model cards, our children begin to choose ways of being that enrich themselves and their world.

The Play

Players mix the deck face down, sending a wish into the cards for guidance on their life path. Then each player chooses nine cards at random. If any court cards appear, these are placed face up and shared with the group.

> Pages/Daughters: Does this remind you of yourself? In what ways do you show the energies of this suit?
> Knights/Sons: Is this what you are becoming? In what ways are you questing for the qualities symbolized in this card?
> Queens/Priestesses, Kings/Shamans: Does this card remind you of any strong adult figure in your life? In what way could this card be a role model for you?

After all the court cards have been shared, players may return all their cards to the pile, mix them, and choose again, until everyone has chosen a court card to explore.

Helping Hand

Fun for two or more, Helping Hand is a cooperative game that teaches children recognition of the suits and the Major Arcana while they enjoy helping one another complete their hands. It gives players a chance to practice asking for what they need and giving freely to others.

The Play

The object of the game is for everyone to end up with a complete hand made up of five cards that they like. A complete hand consists of one card of each suit (Swords, Wands, Cups, and Pentacles) and one card from the Major Arcana.

All players mix the cards, then each person chooses five cards at random, which are placed face up. With the youngest player going first, you may do any one of the following on your turn: (1) If you have more than one of a suit, or if you have more than one Major Arcanum, you may give the extra card to someone who is missing that suit or who has no Major Arcana. Then pick a card from the pile so that you still have at least five cards in your hand; or, (2) ask for what you need and see who will help you out; or, (3) you can put a card back in the pile and choose another. At the end of your turn, you must always have five or more cards in front of you.

Play continues until everyone has completed their hands.

Pathway

This fascinating game plays out the underlying lesson of the cards: We are all involved in the process of reaching milestones as we journey toward wisdom and spiritual development. Pathway is a gentle and cooperative game that visualizes the ways in which we help to complete each other's journey.

Pathway's simplicity makes it an ideal game for children, but adults will enjoy playing it, too.

The Play

The object of this game is to make a pathway leading to a magickal lesson or experience as embodied in the Major Arcana. In order to get there, all players must contribute, and all four suits must be played, since it takes a balance of energies to reach milestones on the path.

All players mix the cards, face down, and then simultaneously choose a card at random. If any positive Major Arcana are drawn, these are placed in a line, in numerical order, with plenty of space left between them. Any less-than-positive Major cards may be placed back in the pile. Players must place one card from each of the four Minor Arcana in between each of the Major cards, in any order they choose. Extra Minor cards may be placed back in the pile.

Players continue choosing cards and placing them in the line. The path may take any form the players like—straight, winding, spiraling. When all four suit cards have been played between any two Major Arcana, the milestone depicted in the second Major Arcana card has been successfully reached. Play may continue until the path reaches the World, the culmination of the Major Arcana, or until you feel that the path is complete.

Here is an example from a game played by students at a small gathering. The last two Major Arcana in the pathway were the Hanged One, which involves transformation resulting from complete surrender, and the Star, which shows great blessings and healing from the higher powers. In order to make the pathway, the following cards were played: the Seven of Pentacles (trusting natural rhythms, not hurrying the process—this player had been fretting over deadlines), the Nine of Swords reversed (shedding negative thoughts that keep the Self bound and unable to move forward—chosen by a young woman with crippling self-esteem issues), the Three of Cups (joyous celebration with like-minded friends—from a player who realized she needed more time to do just that), and the Queen of Wands (positive energy and owning one's own power—which was a much-needed jolt for this player, who had been feeling lethargic). All agreed that blessings and healing were a great place to stop, so the pathway was pronounced complete.

Completing the Circle

Completing the Circle is a great way to encourage cooperative rather than competitive play within a small group.
Children sharpen their creative problem-solving skills when
they work together to make the circle shape, and the beauty of
the cards adds a mysterious and special atmosphere to the play. Adult facilita-
tors may initiate discussion of the cards and their special significance for the
players.

There is a subtle lesson in this game: Not only is each player an important part of the whole circle, but the circle is composed of figures that can be
seen as having differing points of view. Making space for one another's differences is a vital part of life—and we can think of no better image with which to
end the games in this book than that of children helping one another to complete the circle.

The Play

All players mix the cards face down. Then each player chooses six cards,
simultaneously with everyone else and at random, and turns them face up.
The object of the game is for the players to form one circle with all their cards
in the middle of the playing space.

Here is how to do it: Only cards depicting people are used to make the
circle. Any cards that don't have people on them are put back into the pile and
exchanged until people cards are drawn. First, cards with figures who face
straight out in front are placed on the floor in the rough shape of a circle, leaving enough space for two cards to fit between them. Then the spaces must be
filled with cards that show one figure facing to the right and one to the left,

placed so that the figures face each other. Any cards that show two or more people facing in different directions are placed in the center of the circle.

Players must work cooperatively so that all people cards chosen are used and all spaces are filled, completing the circle. This can be difficult to do on the first draw: If the group is unable to complete the circle, players may continue to take turns choosing cards, playing until the circle is complete. If any additional facing-front cards are chosen they are placed in the center of the circle, so that the circle does not continually expand.

Tarot Resources

The world of Tarot resources is becoming so diverse that we cannot even hope to detail its depth and scope here. Instead, what we offer in this section is a selective approach, colored by our own research, discussions, and hands-on Tarot work.

First of all, there are a *lot* of decks out there. Rachel Pollack, in *The New Tarot: Modern Variations of Ancient Images*, has devoted an entire volume to the decks available today—and more are presumably being created even as we write. Pollack herself has produced a marvelous deck based on images from multicultural shrines and holy places that resists being categorized: The Shining Woman deck is both beautiful and powerful. But while we can't give you an exhaustive listing of decks on the market, we can give you a starting place in your quest for the perfect deck by dividing the decks into basic categories. This will give you some idea of the possibilities that exist.

Reproduction decks: These are copies of antique decks, most dating from the eighteenth century, some in French, Italian, or Spanish. We find the reproduction decks very difficult to "see" with, but they have a distinctly occult flavor, and they may appeal to you.

Traditional: These decks are rectangular in shape. We recommend two traditional decks. One is the Rider-Waite, which many people use as a training deck and which is really the jumping-off place for many other traditional decks. It was designed around the turn of the century and contains beautifully complex yet readable symbolism drawn from several systems of mystical knowledge. Our other recommended traditional deck is the Morgan-Greer, which is a variation of the Rider-Waite and uses somewhat juicier colors and images. Many artists have done their own variations of the traditional deck (the Aquarian deck by David Palladino is one example), but most of these seem to lack magick and power. They are visually lovely but without a lot of "oomph." Other examples of artistic traditional decks are the Hanson-Roberts and the Robin Wood, which both have a pale and pretty quality. If you like Art Nouveau, there is an Art Nouveau deck; Salvador Dali fans will enjoy his deck, if they can afford it. There are *many* decks that fit into the traditional category, each with its own slant: Cat People, Tarot of the Witches, the Connolly Tarot, Tarot of the Old Path—let your taste (and your inner voice) be your guide. A word of warning: The Celtic and Arthurian decks, although gorgeous, are not fully pictorial.

Feminist: Many, but not all, of these decks are round in shape. The Motherpeace deck by Vicki Noble and Karen Vogel is not drawn by professional artists, but it simply exudes magick, depth, and power. The figures and colors are strong and vigorous and reflect a respect for other cultures besides the white and Anglo-Saxon. The imagery is transformative and empowering— *highly* recommended. Another example of a feminist deck is the Daughters of the Moon by Ffiona Morgan; it has black-and-white line drawings that you color in yourself (a wonderful way to connect with the cards), and it features positive images of women of all sizes, shapes, races, and ages. A full-color version is also available.

New Age variations: The Inner Child deck by Isha Lerner and Mark Lerner is a wonderful rethinking of the Tarot using the images and symbols of fairy tales. Perfect for use with children (or with this book), the cards themselves are a delight to look at and very healing to use. Another New Age take on the Tarot is the Enchanted Tarot by Amy Zerner and Monte Farber, which includes three levels of meaning for each card.

Native American–inspired: The Medicine Woman deck by Carol Bridges is wonderful—the most positive cards we have ever encountered—but the meanings diverge a bit from traditional interpretations. As with any deck that departs from the traditional, you may find yourself relying on the accompanying booklet to give you the keys you seek, rather than being able to see the answers for yourself. The Native American Tarot deck by Magda Gonzalez and J. A. Gonzalez uses more traditional imagery but with distinctive tribal touches.

Then there are decks that are not Tarot cards at all, but which may be used for some of the games. Lynn Andrews's Power Deck, for instance, is designed for healing of the self and can be a valuable ally. The Medicine Cards by Jamie Sams and David Carson are a collection of Native American–inspired animal totem cards. They will work beautifully for several of the games if the players are familiar with this deck. They won't work for anything involving the suits or the court cards or the Major or Minor Arcana; although this seems to radically limit the possibilities, you can still play Sacred Cave or Snake or many other games with the Medicine Cards and get very powerful results.

Where to find a deck: If your local bookstore carries only a limited selection, your best bet is to shop by catalog. Pyramid Books is a fine resource: You can order their catalog by calling (800) 333-4220. Magickal Childe is another gold mine of Tarot decks and books; they can be contacted at 35 West 19th Street, New York, NY 10011. New Visions Center of York also offers a large mail-order supply source and can be reached at 570 North Belvedere Avenue, York, PA 17404-3112, or call (717) 843-8067.

Further Reading

This selective list will merely whet your appetite. Many of the books included here have more detailed bibliographies—if you've just started learning about Tarot or Goddess spirituality, they will help you continue on your way.

Since we feel very strongly that Circle Games and Tarot used for fortune-telling belong to very different worlds, we have omitted any fortune-telling titles from this section. We have also tried to avoid decks that take this exploitative approach.

We hope that the books included here will move and inspire you, leading you ever deeper as you explore the patterns of connection that link all systems of magickal practice.

On the Tarot

Almond, Jocelyn. *Tarot for Relationships.* San Francisco: Thorsons, 1990.
Arrien, Angeles. *The Tarot Handbook: Practical Applications of Ancient Visual Symbols.* Sonoma, CA: Arcus Publishing, 1987.

Bridges, Carol. *The Medicine Woman Inner Guidebook: A Woman's Guide to Her Unique Powers.* Nashville, IN: Earth Nation Publishing, 1987. This book will become a cherished guide. Highly recommended.

Eakins, Pamela. *Tarot of the Spirit.* New York: Samuel Weiser, 1992.

Fairfield, Gail, and Patti Provo. *Inspiration Tarot: A Workbook for Understanding and Creating Your Own Tarot Deck.* New York: Samuel Weiser, 1991.

Gray, Eden. *A Complete Guide to the Tarot.* New York: Bantam Books, 1972. A good, basic guide to traditional Tarot.

————. *The Tarot Revealed: A Modern Guide to Reading the Tarot Cards.* Revised and updated edition. New York: NAL-Dutton, 1960, 1988.

Greer, Mary K. *Tarot Constellations: Patterns of Personal Destiny.* San Bernardino, CA: Borgo Press, 1988. Fascinating approach to self-understanding.

————. *Tarot Mirrors: Reflections of Personal Meaning.* San Bernardino, CA: Borgo Press, 1988.

————. *Tarot for Yourself: A Workbook for Personal Transformation.* San Bernardino, CA: Borgo Press, 1984.

Jayanti, Amber. *Living the Tarot: Applying the Ancient Oracle to the Challenges of Modern Life.* San Bernardino, CA: Borgo Press, 1988.

Knight, Gareth. *Tarot and Magic: Images for Ritual and Pathworking.* Rochester, VT: Inner Tradition, 1991.

Morgan, Frederick. *The Tarot of Cornelius Agrippa.* Sand Lake, NY: Sagarin Press, 1971. This magickal little book, long out of print, is well worth the search. The book is made up of short, evocative stories based on each of the Major Arcana. Try reading them before you go to sleep and see what dreams you get!

Nichols, Sallie. *Jung and Tarot: An Archetypal Journey.* New York: Samuel Weiser, 1984.

Noble, Vicki. *Motherpeace: A Way to the Goddess through Myth, Art, and Tarot.* San Francisco: Harper & Row, 1983. Highly recommended. Transformative and powerful, a feminist rethinking of the Tarot.

Noble, Vicki, and Jonathan Tenney. *The Motherpeace Tarot Playbook: Astrology and the Motherpeace Cards.* Berkeley: Wingbow Press, 1986. Explores the connection between Tarot and astrology.

Peach, Emily. *Tarot Workbook: Understanding and Using Tarot Symbolism.* New York: Sterling, 1985.

Pollack, Rachel. *The New Tarot: Modern Variations of Ancient Images.* Woodstock, NY: Overlook Press, 1992.

———. *Seventy-Eight Degrees of Wisdom: A Book of Tarot: An in-depth analysis of the symbolism and psychological resonances of the Tarot suit cards, including instructions on how to give readings.* London: Aquarian Press, 1983. A must for a greater in-depth understanding of the cards.

———. *Tarot Readings and Meditations: How the Tarot can help us answer specific questions, act as a tool for psychological analysis, and tell us how to overcome problems.* London: Aquarian Press, 1986. Enlightened, sensitive, and intelligent.

Stuart, Micheline. *The Tarot Path to Self-Development.* Boston: Shambhala Publications, 1990.

Waite, Arthur E. *A Pictorial Key to the Tarot.* New York: Citadel Press, 1979.

The Goddess, Women's Spirituality, Correspondences, Protection Work, Seasonal Rituals, and More

Beck, Renee, and Sydney Barbara Metrick. *The Art of Ritual.* Berkeley: Celestial Arts, 1990.

Budapest, Z. *Grandmother Moon: Lunar Magic in Our Lives.* San Francisco: HarperSanFrancisco, 1991.

———. *The Grandmother of Time.* San Francisco: HarperSanFrancisco, 1989.

———. *The Holy Book of Women's Mysteries.* Vols. 1 and 2. Revised. Berkeley: Wingbow Press, 1986.

Campanelli, Pauline. *Ancient Ways: Reclaiming Pagan Traditions.* St. Paul,

MN: Llewellyn Publications, 1991. Full of inspiring, spiritually nourishing ideas for honoring and celebrating the seasons.

———. *Wheel of the Year: Living the Magickal Life.* St. Paul, MN: Llewellyn Publications, 1987. Both this and *Ancient Ways* are valuable resources for planning seasonal rituals and activities.

Eisler, Riane. *The Chalice and the Blade: Our History, Our Future.* San Francisco: HarperSanFrancisco, 1986. Excellent, visionary, and inspiring.

Eisler, Riane, and David Loye. *The Partnership Way: New Tools for Living and Learning, Healing Our Families, Our Communities, and Our World.* San Francisco: HarperSanFrancisco, 1990.

Estés, Clarissa Pinkola. *Women Who Run with the Wolves: Myths and Stories of the Wild Woman Archetype.* New York: Ballantine Books, 1992.

Gawain, Shakti. *Creative Visualization.* Mill Valley, CA: Whatever Publishing, 1978.

Mariechild, Diane. *Mother Wit: A Guide to Healing and Psychic Development.* Freedom, CA: Crossing Press, 1988. This second edition of her groundbreaking book is even better than the original. Wonderful meditations for healing and deepening. Highly recommended.

Noble, Vicki. *Shakti Woman: Feeling Our Fire, Healing Our World: The New Female Shamanism.* San Francisco: HarperSanFrancisco, 1991.

———. *Uncoiling the Snake: Ancient Patterns in Contemporary Women's Lives.* San Francisco: HarperSanFrancisco, 1993.

Starhawk. *Dreaming the Dark: Magic, Sex, and Politics.* Boston: Beacon Press, 1982.

———. *The Spiral Dance: A Rebirth of the Ancient Religion of the Great Goddess: Rituals, Invocations, Exercises, Magic.* San Francisco: Harper & Row, 1989. This tenth anniversary edition of Starhawk's groundbreaking work is the first book we recommend for anyone interested in Goddess spirituality. After you've read it, you'll know why we named one of our Circle Games in honor of this author.

———. *Truth or Dare.* San Francisco: Harper Collins, 1989.

Stein, Diane. *The Women's Spirituality Book.* St. Paul, MN: Llewellyn Publications, 1987. Filled with valuable information and beautiful artwork.

Stone, Merlin. *When God Was a Woman.* New York: Harcourt Brace Jovanovich, 1978. Well researched and a delight to read; a good introduction to the diversity and power of our ancient Goddess heritage.

Teish, Luisa. *Jambalaya: The Natural Woman's Book of Personal Charms and Practical Rituals.* San Francisco: Harper & Row, 1985.

Walker, Barbara G. *The Secrets of the Tarot: Origins, History, and Symbolism.* San Francisco: Harper & Row, 1984.

————. *The Woman's Encyclopedia of Myths and Secrets.* San Francisco: Harper & Row, 1983.

Weinstein, Marion. *Earth Magic: A Dianic Book of Shadows.* Custer, WA: Phoenix Publishing, 1986.

————. *Positive Magic: Occult Self-Help.* Custer, WA: Phoenix Publishing, 1984.

Worth, Valerie. *The Crone's Book of Words.* St. Paul, MN: Llewellyn Publications, 1986.

Also Not to Be Missed

SageWoman, a quarterly magazine of women's spirituality, is a longtime favorite. Filled with inspirational and informative articles, artwork, poetry, and features (including one on Tarot), *SageWoman* is a delight to read and treasure. The ads list dozens of great sources for Tarot decks, books, and magickal goodies of all kinds. For information, write to P.O. Box 641, Point Arena, CA 95468.

Maiden, Mother, Crone: The Goddess in Our Lives is a new quarterly magazine that promises to be a rich and wonderful trove of Goddess-goodies. Contact the editors at 8 Laurel Park Road, Wappingers Falls, NY 12590.

If you want more information on networking with others on the Nature Spirit path, write to CIRCLE at P.O. Box 219, Mt. Horeb, WI 53572. CIRCLE publishes a quarterly newspaper, *Circle Network News,* that is an invaluable resource.

And for parents and caregivers, *Mothering* magazine gives wonderful support and has a wealth of information on nurturing and raising our children in a heart-centered way. Write to P.O. Box 532, Mt. Morris, IL 61054-7856.

Acknowledgments

First, we would like to thank Vicki Noble, whose work literally has transformed us. We are deeply honored by her Preface to this book. Our thanks also to artist Durga Bernhard and designer Jaime Robles—their powerful artwork and sensitive design have made our book so beautiful. And thanks to Barbara Moulton, our editor, for her willingness to explore the deep magick of the Tarot, and whose insistence on clarity has strengthened our work. Thanks also to Lisa Bach, senior editorial assistant at Harper San Francisco, who always has a ready laugh and the answer to every question.

I want to thank my coauthor, Maura, whose sudden, miraculous appearance in my life was a gift straight from the Goddess we both serve. Besides being a continual source of delight, she has become essential to my life. It is a blessing to know her. My life companion, Stuart Hannan, has quietly and consistently given me his support, both material and emotional. In this project, as in so much, he gave me the grounding I needed. Our son, Reid, by simply being, surrounding me always with his wonderful sense of humor and fun, and by serving as willing guinea pig for the children's games, has contributed greatly to the children's section of the book. My parents, Pat and Bob Johnson, have been warmly supportive of this project. I learned from them the pleasure of keeping our inner children alive as a playful source of inspiration. And my gratitude always to the spirit of my grandmother, Elizabeth Johnson, whose death just as Maura and I began this book was such a painful loss, but whose presence has been and continues to be a deep influence in my life. Finally, I want to thank my sisters: sisters of the Circle, sisters of the heart, teachers, healers, compassionate friends, whose wisdom and courage and love have filled my life with a very real sense of community.

Cait Johnson

Perhaps it is a bit unusual for coauthors to thank one another for their work together, but my gratitude to Cait extends far beyond the creation of this book, which is the child of her playful, inventive spirit. When we began our writing partnership we were strangers to each other, alternately sharing the roles of student and teacher; now we have become the dearest of friends. Cait drew me into the Circle and gently, at my own pace, allowed me to reconnect with the Goddess and take back the strong female voice that I had lost in some distant past. To my wonderful friend Joyce Townsend—surely my sister in another life—I offer thanks for dragging me off to the Tarot workshop where I first met Cait. By ignoring my pleas for a quiet, restful evening, Joyce ensured that I would be busy for the rest of my life. From the depth of my heart I want to thank my husband, Joe Tantillo, for being always already there—no matter where my path winds. And thanks to our son, Nick, who is an enthusiastic companion in my searches for new

Tarot decks, books, crystals, and incense, although he is not overly fond of mugwort tea. My mother, Bev Shaw, understands the joy of creative work and has shared it with me since my earliest years. To my friends, colleagues, and students who have so willingly played the games—sometimes their first encounters with the Tarot—I express appreciation for their trust and belief in me. It is my hope that the spirit of love and community that Cait and I tried to instill in this book will bring blessings to all.

Maura D. Shaw

About the Authors

Cait Johnson has been actively involved in the reclamation of Goddess-centered spirituality for many years. She has founded Full Moon circles for women and facilitates workshops here and abroad on the Tarot, women's rituals, dreamwork, and earth-based creativity. She is a mother, writer, artist, and Tarot counselor, who works with the cards to help people better understand and transform their lives. She lives in the Hudson Valley with her partner and their son, where she is presently completing her first novel.

Maura D. Shaw is a writer and editor who has worked for nearly twenty years in scholarly publishing. Formerly managing editor of the Yale University Press and the *Journal of the History of Sexuality*, she came to the path of women's spirituality and Goddess-consciousness through her commitment to feminism and women's issues. In her classes she uses the Tarot as a healing tool to access inner wisdom; in her writing, both fiction and nonfiction, she tries to awaken women to the power within them. She lives in Wappingers Falls, New York, with her husband and son.

Made in the USA
Las Vegas, NV
31 January 2023

66572811R00077